AVICENNA ON THEOLOGY

Avicenna on Theology

By

ARTHUR J. ARBERRY, Litt.D., F.B.A.

Fellow of Pembroke College and
Sir Thomas Adams's Professor of Arabic
in the University of Cambridge

HYPERION PRESS, INC.
Westport, Connecticut

Published in 1951 by J. Murray, London
Hyperion reprint edition 1979
Library of Congress Catalog Number 78-59000
ISBN 0-88355-676-6
Printed in the United States of America

Library of Congress Cataloging in Publication Data
Avicenna, 980-1037.
    Avicenna on theology.
    Reprint of the 1951 ed. published by J. Murray,
London, in the Wisdom of the East series.
    Includes index.
    1. Islamic theology—Early works to 1800.
2. Avicenna, 980-1037. 3. Muslims—Biography.
I. Arberry, Arthur John, 1905-1969.   II. Title.
III. Series: The Wisdom of the East series.
[BP166.A92   1979]   297'.2   78-59000
ISBN 0-88355-676-6

CONTENTS

INTRODUCTION

THE year 1951 is being celebrated throughout the Muslim world, and especially in Persia, as the millennary according to lunar reckoning of the birth of Avicenna, one of the greatest and most original thinkers produced by Islam. Born in 370 (980) at the little village of Afshana in the province of Bukhara—a region now hopelessly lost within the territories of the Soviet empire —Abū 'Alī al-Ḥusain ibn 'Abd Allāh called Ibn Sīnā (to give him his Muslim name) largely by virtue of his own exceptional genius and diligent self-instruction became a master alike of the ancient Greek learning and the Arab sciences, and was the author of large works on medicine and philosophy which, translated into Latin, continued to be studied in the medieval universities of Europe to the end of the sixteenth century.

Concerning Avicenna's genealogy we know virtually nothing. His father 'Abd Allāh, a native of Balkh, was appointed governor of an outlying district of Bukhara by the Samanid ruler Nūḥ II ibn Manṣūr, and was therefore presumably a man of some substance ; his grandfather's name was al-Ḥasan, his great-grandfather's name was 'Alī, but that is all history records of them. How he came to be called Ibn Sīnā is entirely obscure : it has been fancifully supposed that the name indicates a Chinese origin, but the word for Chinese in Arabic is spelt with a different kind of s. The region of Transoxania, territories over which the Samanid dynasty reigned, certainly had a very mixed population in the tenth century A.D. ; lying within the broad area of Iranian occupation since pre-history, it had been the scene of repeated struggles against invading Turkish tribes, long before the Arab legions carried Islam into an expanse once extensively Buddhist. It thus arises that Arabs, Persians and Turks all claim Avicenna as a compatriot; at this point of history, with the scanty information at our disposal, it is impossible to pass final judgment on the merits of these rival pretensions. But it can almost certainly be said that Avicenna had at least a half-share of Persian blood in him, for his mother's name was Sitāra, which in Persian means "star".

If our knowledge of Avicenna's ancestry and nationality is thus meagre, we are fortunate in possessing comparatively excellent sources for reconstructing his biography. For his early years we are able to rely upon his own autobiography as recorded by his pupil Abū 'Ubaid al-Jūzjānī, and quoted by the Arab historians of philosophy and medicine, al-Qiftī (d. 1248) and Ibn Abī Uṣaibi'a (d. 1270); the story of his later life has been written by the same al-Jūzjānī and preserved by the same authorities. These first-hand documents have been translated and appended to this introduction. Other secondary sources confirm the facts presented in these two accounts, and add further illustrative details.

A brief summary of the political history of Persia during Avicenna's lifetime is necessary, to indicate the somewhat confused and unsettled circumstances under which he worked and wrote. Though nominally part of the vast empire ruled over by the caliphs of Baghdad, these territories since early in the ninth century had been directly governed by virtually independent princes, under whom the old proud spirit, and with it the rich and varied culture of Iran, crushed by the stunning shock of the Arab conquest, was now reviving. Bukhara itself was the capital of the Samanid amirs; the first seventeen years of Avicenna's life were passed under Nūh II, whose reign was disturbed by frequent insurrections and brushes with neighbouring principalities, and saw the rise to power of the Turkish slave Subuktagīn, father of the famous Maḥmūd of Ghazna. After Nūḥ's death in 997 the Samanid kingdom rapidly broke up, the dynasty coming to an end in 999 when Maḥmūd the Ghaznavid overran its remaining territories.

This catastrophe marked the beginning of Avicenna's wanderings, fortunately not before the precocious youth had made himself master of many sciences and acquired that encyclopaedic knowledge upon which his later original achievements were securely based. Though Maḥmūd was eager to add him to the galaxy of talent and learning which he was pleased to have illuminate his court, the philosopher preferred to throw in his lot with Persian princes rather than risk the capricious patronage of the fanatical Turkish *parvenu*.

Avicenna's first refuge was Gurganj (Jurjaniya) in northern Khwarizm, the ruler of which had lately succeeded in reuniting the whole province under one throne, thus refounding the brilliant regime of the Khwārizmshāhs. But he did not feel settled there, having in mind, as he tells us, to join the service of Qābūs ibn Washmgīr, the Ziyarid prince of Tabaristan, who in 998 regained his throne after long exile, only to lose it in 1012 before the philosopher could come to him. After extended wanderings Avicenna eventually came to rest in Raiy, the capital of the eastern Buyid ruler Majd al-Daula ; his stay was not prolonged, however, for the Buyid house, once great and powerful, was now rent by family quarrels and a ready prey to adventurous rebels and more vigorous neighbours.

He next tried his luck at Hamadhan, and found favour with Shams al-Daula, the brother and rival of his former protector Majd al-Daula. Shams al-Daula had seized power in 1015, and enjoyed his throne until 1022 ; during these years Avicenna was held in high favour at the court of Hamadhan, being twice

appointed vizier. Shams al-Daula's son on succeeding to the
rulership would have continued Avicenna in office ; but the
philosopher, no doubt diagnosing the mortal sickness of the
regime and foreseeing its early demise, began secret overtures
to transfer his allegiance to the Kakuyid ruler 'Alā' al-Daula,
who from his capital Isfahan was plotting the overthrow of the
Buyids of Hamadhan. Avicenna was thrown into prison by
Tāj al-Mulk, who however after suffering defeat at the hands
of 'Alā'al-Daula sought to make his peace with him ; but one
night the great philosopher escaped in Sufi disguise and succeeded
in making his way to Isfahan, his final refuge. It was in 'Alā'
al-Daula's service that he ended his days in 428 (1037).

Politics have always been closely interwoven with theology
in the pattern of the Islamic state ; the fortunes of princes during
Avicenna's lifetime were but facets of the wider struggle between
orthodoxy and schism. The caliphate of Baghdad was Sunnī,
and the days were long past when the liberal Ma'mūn (d. 813),
great patron of Greek learning, could nominate as his successor
a Shī'ite imam. Mutawakkil (d. 847), under the influence of
his fundamentalist ulema, encouraged a reaction against all
foreign influences in Islam. Shī'ism, in retreat at the capital,
took refuge with the semi-independent courts of the Samanids
and the Buyids ; the Fatimids, establishing themselves in Cairo,
secretly plotted the overthrow of the orthodox caliphs of Islam
and sent their Ismā'ilī propagandists as far afield as distant
Transoxania. The mystical doctrine of the hereditary Imamate,
the theory of that divine light which was transmitted through
the lineal descendants of the Prophet—a notion itself closely
related to the old Persian legend of the royal splendour—found
welcome support in the fantastic speculations of the later Hellenistic philosophers. In the celebrated *Epistles of the Brethren of
Purity*, circulated during the last quarter of the tenth century

in order to win sympathy for ultra-Shī'ite political pretensions, a bold attempt was made to reconcile an allegorized Islamic theology with Neo-pythagorean, Gnostic and Hermetic notions which were the principal constituents of a characteristic oriental syncretism.

Avicenna seems almost certainly to have belonged to a Shī'ite family ; though this is not a decisive argument, all the names of his household known to us were popular in Shī'ite circles ; his father, according to the autobiography, became converted to Ismā'īlism. Nūḥ II was a Shī'ite sympathizer, and we read with great interest of the magnificent Samanid library to which the youthful Avicenna had access ; this vast repository, later destroyed—no doubt by those Sunni zealots who did not scruple to whisper that the torch which fired the treasury of learning was lit by the philosopher himself, jealous to keep to himself knowledge he had there imbibed—contained many manuscripts of Greek science not available elsewhere. Avicenna rejected with scorn the mumbled mysteries of Ismā'īlī propaganda, but made his own attempt to reconcile Islamic doctrine with Greek philosophy, uncontaminated by irrational " wisdom " accretions.

The fame of Avicenna rests chiefly upon his two greatest books. The Qānūn, his comprehensive treatise on medicine, translated into Latin in the twelfth century, became the chief textbook of medical studies in medieval Europe and figured in university curricula for five hundred years. His Shifā', an encyclopaedia of Aristotelian philosophy and science with many original addenda, proved scarcely less influential in the history of human thought. The present little volume does not pretend to estimate Avicenna's contribution to medicine and science, and is concerned with his philosophy only to a very limited extent ; its chief object is to isolate from the great mass of his writings some aspects of his theological speculation.

Even during his lifetime Avicenna was suspected of infidelity to Islam ; after his death accusations of heresy, freethought and atheism were repeatedly levelled against him. The battle between free speculation and orthodox belief was decisively won by his great compatriot Ghazālī (d. 1111), whose *Tahāfut al-falāsifa* (" Incoherence of the Philosophers ") ended forever any possibility that Avicenna's system might provide the pattern for a broader Islamic theology.

It is not possible within the scope of this brief essay to discuss all the points of dispute between Avicenna and the orthodox. Some of the charges brought against him were obviously untrue, so far at least as a non-Muslim may presume to judge. He certainly believed in One God ; he certainly accepted the doctrine of prophetic inspiration, and the authority of Muhammad as the lawgiver of Islam ; he both practised, and defended on theoretical grounds, the ritual worship and religious obligations of his faith. But it cannot be denied that for him, as for the Greeks of old whose writings he knew so well, God's highest gift to man was not faith but reason. And on one most important point of doctrine he was unquestionably, gloriously heretical : he rejected unreservedly the resurrection of the body, and with it the literal acceptance of those passages in the Koran describing in graphic physical terms the pleasures of paradise and the tortures of the damned. For him, as for the Neoplatonists, the supreme reward of virtue, the purest felicity attainable by man, was the intellectual apprehension of God. A thousand years have gone by since he threw down the challenge, and never in Islam or Christianity has the paradox of a physical resurrection been more boldly or more forlornly exploded.

To read Avicenna on theology, as the attempt has been made to present him in the following pages, is to be aware of standing in the presence of one of the profoundest and most courageous thinkers in history. He was a Muslim, and the crown of his achievement as a speculative philosopher was to extend Aristotelian metaphysics, as interpreted by the Hellenistic commentators, so as to embrace the fundamental doctrines and practices of the religion he professed. His arguments required but little elaboration to adapt them to an equally powerful defence of basic Christianity and Judaism. So far as the present writer can see, his case for a reasoned monotheism, for the immortality of the soul, and for the lofty beatitude of intellectual contemplation, is not unacceptable even to-day, a millennium after he was born. Surely his greatness needs no further advertisement.

AUTOBIOGRAPHY OF AVICENNA

MY father was a man of Balkh, and he moved from there to Bukhara during the days of Nūḥ ibn Manṣūr ; in his reign he was employed in the administration, being governor of a village-centre in the outlying district of Bukhara called Kharmaithan. Near by is a village named Afshana, and there my father married my mother and took up his residence; I was also born there, and after me my brother. Later we moved to Bukhara, where I was put under teachers of the Koran and of letters. By the time I was ten I had mastered the Koran and a great deal of literature, so that I was marvelled at for my aptitude.

Now my father was one of those who had responded to the Egyptian propagandist (who was an Ismaili) ; he, and my brother too, had listened to what they had to say about the Spirit and the Intellect, after the fashion in which they preach and understand the matter. They would therefore discuss these things together, while I listened and comprehended all that they said ; but my spirit would not assent to their argument. Presently they began to invite me to join the movement, rolling on their tongues talk about philosophy, geometry, Indian arithmetic ; and my father sent me to a certain vegetable-seller who used the Indian arithmetic, so that I might learn it from him. Then there came to Bukhara a man called Abū 'Abd Allāh al-Nātilī who claimed to be a philosopher ; my father invited him to stay in our house, hoping that I would learn from him also. Before his advent I had already occupied myself with Muslim jurisprudence, attending Ismā'il the Ascetic ; so I was an excellent enquirer, having become familiar with the methods

9

of postulation and the techniques of rebuttal according to the
usages of the canon lawyers. I now commenced reading the
Isagoge (of Porphyry) with al-Nātilī : when he mentioned to
me the definition of *genus* as a term applied to a number of things
of different species in answer to the question " What is it ? "
I set about verifying this definition in a manner such as he had
never heard. He marvelled at me exceedingly, and warned my
father that I should not engage in any other occupation but
learning ; whatever problem he stated to me, I showed a better
mental conception of it than he. So I continued until I had read
all the straightforward parts of Logic with him ; as for the
subtler points, he had no acquaintance with them.

From then onward I took to reading texts by myself; I
studied the commentaries, until I had completely mastered the
science of Logic. Similarly with Euclid I read the first five
or six figures with him, and thereafter undertook on my own
account to solve the entire remainder of the book. Next I
moved on to the *Almagest* (of Ptolemy) ; when I had finished
the prolegomena and reached the geometrical figures, al-Nātilī
told me to go on reading and to solve the problems by myself ;
I should merely revise what I read with him, so that he might
indicate to me what was right and what was wrong. The
truth is that he did not really teach this book ; I began to solve
the work, and many were the complicated figures of which he
had no knowledge until I presented them to him, and made
him understand them. Then al-Nātilī took leave of me, setting
out for Gurganj.

I now occupied myself with mastering the various texts and
commentaries on natural science and metaphysics, until all the
gates of knowledge were open to me. Next I desired to study
medicine, and proceeded to read all the books that have been
written on this subject. Medicine is not a difficult science, and

naturally I excelled in it in a very short time, so that qualified physicians began to read medicine with me. I also undertook to treat the sick, and methods of treatment derived from practical experience revealed themselves to me such as baffle description. At the same time I continued between whiles to study and dispute on law, being now sixteen years of age.

The next eighteen months I devoted entirely to reading; I studied Logic once again, and all the parts of philosophy. During all this time I did not sleep one night through, nor devoted my attention to any other matter by day. I prepared a set of files; with each proof I examined, I set down the syllogistic premisses and put them in order in the files, then I examined what deductions might be drawn from them. I observed methodically the conditions of the premisses, and proceeded until the truth of each particular problem was confirmed for me. Whenever I found myself perplexed by a problem, or could not find the middle term in any syllogism, I would repair to the mosque and pray, adoring the All-Creator, until my puzzle was resolved and my difficulty made easy. At night I would return home, set the lamp before me, and busy myself with reading and writing; whenever sleep overcame me or I was conscious of some weakness, I turned aside to drink a glass of wine until my strength returned to me; then I went back to my reading. If ever the least slumber overtook me, I would dream of the precise problem which I was considering as I fell asleep; in that way many problems revealed themselves to me while sleeping. So I continued until I had made myself master of all the sciences; I now comprehended them to the limits of human possibility. All that I learned during that time is exactly as I know it now; I have added nothing more to my knowledge to this day.

I was now a master of Logic, natural sciences and mathematics. I therefore returned to metaphysics ; I read the *Meta-physica* (of Aristotle), but did not understand its contents and was baffled by the author's intention ; I read it over forty times, until I had the text by heart. Even then I did not understand it or what the author meant, and I despaired within myself, saying, " This is a book which there is no way of understanding." But one day at noon I chanced to be in the booksellers' quarter, and a broker was there with a volume in his hand which he was calling for sale. He offered it to me, but I returned it to him impatiently, believing that there was no use in this particular science. However he said to me, " Buy this book from me : it is cheap, and I will sell it to you for four dirhams. The owner is in need of the money." So I bought it, and found that it was a book by Abū Naṣr al-Fārābī *On the Objects of the Metaphysica.* I returned home and hastened to read it ; and at once the objects of that book became clear to me, for I had it all by heart. I rejoiced at this, and upon the next day distributed much in alms to the poor in gratitude to Almighty God.

Now the Sultan of Bukhara at that time was Nūḥ ibn Manṣūr, and it happened that he fell sick of a malady which baffled all the physicians. My name was famous among them because of the breadth of my reading ; they therefore mentioned me in his presence, and begged him to summon me. I attended the sick-room, and collaborated with them in treating the royal patient. So I came to be enrolled in his service. One day I asked his leave to enter their library, to examine the contents and read the books on medicine ; he granted my request, and I entered a mansion with many chambers, each chamber having chests of books piled one upon another. In one apartment were books on language and poetry, in another law, and so on ; each apartment was set aside for books on a single science. I glanced through the catalogue of the works of the ancient Greeks, and asked for those which I required ; and I saw books whose very names are as yet unknown to many—works which I had never seen before and have not seen since. I read these books, taking notes of their contents ; I came to realize the place each man occupied in his particular science.

So by the time I reached my eighteenth year I had exhausted all these sciences. My memory for learning was at that period of my life better than it is now, but to-day I am more mature ; apart from this my knowledge is exactly the same, nothing further having been added to my store since then.

There lived near me in those days a man called Abu 'l-Ḥasan the Prosodist ; he requested me to compose a comprehensive work on this science, and I wrote for him the *Majmū'* (" Compendium ") which I named after him, including in it all the branches of knowledge except mathematics. At that time I was twenty-one. Another man lived in my neighbourhood called Abū Bakr al-Barqī, a Khwarizmian by birth ; he was a lawyer at heart, his interests being focused on jurisprudence, exegesis and asceticism, to which subjects he was extremely inclined. He asked me to comment on his books, and I wrote for him *al-Ḥāṣil wa'l-maḥṣūl* (" The Import and the Substance ") in about twenty volumes, as well as a work on ethics called *al-Birr wa'l-ithm* (" Good Works and Sin ") ; these two books are only to be found in his library, and are unknown to anyone else, so that they have never been copied.

Then my father died, and my circumstances changed. I accepted a post in the Sultan's employment, and was obliged to move from Bukhara to Gurganj, where Abu 'l-Ḥusain al-Sahlī was a minister, being a man devoted to these sciences. I was introduced to the Amir, 'Alī ibn al-Ma'mūn, being at that time dressed in the garb of lawyers, with scarf and chin-wrap ; they fixed a handsome salary for me, amply sufficient for the like of me.   Then I was constrained to move to Nasa, and from there to Baward, and thence successively to Tus, Shaqqan, Samanqan, Jajarm the frontier-post of Khurasan, and Jurjan.   My entire purpose was to come to the Amir Qābūs ; but it happened meanwhile that Qābūs was taken and imprisoned in a fortress, where he died.

After this I went to Dihistan, where I fell very ill.   I returned to Jurjan, and there made friends with Abū 'Ubaid al-Jūzjānī.

BIOGRAPHY OF AVICENNA

By Abū 'Ubaid al-Jūzjānī

(In continuation of the " Autobiography ")

FROM this point I mention those episodes of the Master's life of which I was myself a witness during my association with him, up to the time of his death.

There was at Jurjan a man called Abū Muḥammad al-Shīrāzī, who loved these sciences ; he had bought for the Master a house near where he lived, and lodged him there. I used to visit him every day, reading the *Almagest* and listening to him lecturing on Logic ; he dictated to me *al-Mukhtaṣar al-ausat* (" The Middle Summary ") on that subject. For Abū Muḥammad al-Shīrāzī he composed *al-Mabda' wa'l-ma'ād* (" The Origin and the Return ") and *al-Arṣād al-kullīya* (" The General Observations "). He wrote many books there, such as the first part of *al-Qānūn* (" The Canon "), the *Mukhtaṣar al-Majistī* (" Summary of Almagest ") and many essays. Then he composed in the Jebel country the rest of his books.

After this the Master removed to Raiy, where he joined the service of al-Saiyida and her son Majd al-Daula ; they knew of him because of the many letters he brought with him containing appreciations of his worth. At that time Majd al-Daula was overcome by melancholy, and the Master applied himself to treating him. At Raiy he composed the *Kitāb al-Ma'ād* (" Book of the Return "), staying there until Shams al-Daula attacked the city following the slaying of Hilāl ibn Badr ibn Ḥasanawaih and the rout of the Baghdad army. Thereafter

15

circumstances conspired to oblige him to leave Raiy for Qazwin, and from Qazwin he proceeded to Hamadhan, where he entered the service of Kadhbānūya in order to investigate her finances. Shams al-Daula then became acquainted with him, and summoned him to his court because of an attack of colic which had afflicted him ; he treated him, until God cured him of the sickness, and he departed from his palace loaded with many costly robes. So he returned home, having passed forty days and nights at the palace and become one of the Amir's intimates.

Now it came to pass that the Amir went up to Qarmisin, to make war on 'Anāz, the Master accompanying him ; but he was routed, and returned to Hamadhan. They then asked him to take the office of vizier, and he accepted ; but the army conspired against him, fearing for themselves on his account ; they surrounded his house, haled him off to prison, pillaged his belongings, and took all that he possessed. They even demanded of the Amir that he should put him to death, but this he refused, though he was agreeable to banishing him from the State, being anxious to conciliate them. The Master concealed himself for forty days in the house of Abū Sa'd ibn Dakhdūk ; at the end of which time Shams al-Daula was again attacked by colic, and sent for him. He came to court, and the Amir apologized to him profoundly ; so the Master applied himself to treating him. As a result he continued in honour and high consideration at court, and was appointed vizier a second time.

Then it was that I asked him to write a commentary on the works of Aristotle ; but he remarked that he had not the leisure at that time, adding, " If you will be satisfied for me to compose a book setting forth the parts of those sciences which I believe to be sound, not disputing therein with any opponents nor troubling to reply to their arguments, I will gladly do so." This offer I accepted, and he began work on the physical sections of the *Kitāb al-Shifā'* ("Book of the Remedy"). He had already composed the first book of the *Qānūn*; and every night students gathered in his house, and by turns I would read the *Shifā'* and another the *Qānūn*. When we had finished the allotted portion the various musicians would enter; vessels were brought out for a drinking party; and so we occupied ourselves. The studying was done by night because during the day his attendance upon the Amir left him no spare time.

We continued after this fashion for some while. Then the Amir set out for Tarm, to fight the prince of that place. Upon this expedition the colic again visited the Amir near Tarm; the attack was severe, and was aggravated by complications brought on by his irregular habits and his disinclination to follow the Master's advice. The army feared he would die, and at once returned towards Hamadhan carrying him in a cradle, but he died on the way. Shams al-Daula's son was thereupon sworn in as Amir, and the army now requested that the Master should be appointed vizier, but this he declined; he corresponded in secret with 'Alā' al-Daula, seeking to come to his court and join his service. Meanwhile he remained in hiding in the house of Abū Ghālib the Druggist. I requested him to complete the *Shifā'*, and he summoned Abū Ghālib and asked for paper and ink; these being brought, the Master wrote in about twenty parts (each having eight folios) in his own hand the main topics to be discussed; in two days he had drafted all the topics, without having any book at hand or source to consult, accomplishing the work entirely from memory. Then he placed these parts before him, took paper, and began to examine each topic and write his comments on it. Each day he wrote fifty leaves, until he had completed the natural sciences and metaphysics save for the books of zoology and botany. He commenced work on the logic, and wrote one part of this; but then Tāj al-Mulk suspected him of corresponding with 'Alā' al-Daula, and disapproving of this instituted a search for him. The Master's whereabouts were betrayed by an enemy, and he was committed to a fortress called Fardjan, where he remained for four months.

Then 'Alā' al-Daula attacked and captured Hamadhan ; Tāj al-Mulk was routed, and passed into the very same fortress. Presently 'Alā' al-Daula withdrew from Hamadhan ; Tāj al-Mulk and the son of Shams al-Daula returned, carrying with them the Master, who took up his lodging in the house of al-'Alawī and busied himself with composing the logic of the *Shifā'*. While imprisoned in the fortress he had written the *Kitāb al-Hidāya* (" Book of Guidance "), the *Risāla Haiy ibn Yaqzān* (" Treatise of Living the Son of Wakeful ") and the *Kitāb al-Qūlanj* (" Book of Colic ") : as for *al-Adwiyat al-qalbīya* (" The Cardiac Remedies "), this he composed when he first came to Hamadhan.

So some time elapsed, and Tāj al-Mulk was all the while encouraging him with handsome promises. Then it seemed good to the Master to betake himself to Isfahan ; he went forth in disguise, accompanied by myself, his brother and two slaves, in the habit of Sufis, and so we reached Tabaran at the gate of Isfahan, having suffered great hardships on the way. Friends of the Master, and courtiers of 'Alā' al-Daula came out to welcome him ; robes were brought, and fine equipages, and he was lodged in a quarter called Gun-Gunbadh at the house of 'Abd Allāh b. Bābā ; his apartment was furnished and carpeted in the most ample manner. At court he was received with the respect and consideration which he so richly merited ; and 'Alā' al-Daula appointed every Friday night a meeting for learned discussion before him, to be attended by all the scholars according to their various degrees, the Master Abū 'Alī among them ;

in these gatherings he proved himself quite supreme and unrivalled in every branch of learning.

At Isfahan he set about completing the *Shifā'* ; he finished the logic and the *Almagest*, and had already epitomized Euclid, the arithmetic and the music. In each book of the mathematical section he introduced supplementary materials as he thought to be necessary ; in the *Almagest* he brought up ten new figures on various points of speculation, and in the astronomical section at the end of that work he added things which had never been discovered before. In the same way he introduced some new examples into Euclid, enlarged the arithmetic with a number of excellent refinements, and discussed problems on music which the ancient Greeks had wholly neglected. So he finished the *Shifā'*, all but the botany and zoology which he composed in the year when 'Alā' al-Daula marched to Sabur-Khwast ; these parts he wrote *en route*, as well as the *Kitāb al-Najāt* (" Book of Deliverance ").

The Master had now become one of the intimate courtiers of 'Alā' al-Daula. When the latter determined to attack Hamadhan, the Master accompanied him ; and one night a discussion took place in the Amir's presence concerning the imperfections that occur in the astronomical tables according to the observations of the ancients. The Amir commanded the Master to undertake observations of the stars, supplying him with all the funds he might require ; so he began this new work, deputing me to select the instruments and engage the skilled assistants needed. So many old problems were elucidated, it being found that the imperfections in the former observations were due to their being conducted in the course of many journeys, with all the impediments resulting therefrom.

At Isfahan the Master also wrote the *'Alā'ī* (an encyclopaedia named after 'Alā' al-Daula). Now one of the remarkable things about the Master was, that during the twenty-five years I accompanied and served him I never saw him take a new book and read it right through ; he looked always for the difficult passages and complicated problems and examined what the author had said on these, so as to discover what his degree of learning and level of understanding might be.

One day the Master was seated before the Amir, and Abū Manṣūr al-Jabbān was also present. A philological problem came up for discussion ; the Master gave his views as they occurred to him, whereupon Abū Manṣūr turned to him and remarked, " You are a philosopher and a wise man ; but you have never studied philology to such an extent that we should be pleased to hear you discourse on the subject." The Master was stung by this rebuke, and devoted the next three years to studying books on philology ; he even sent for the *Tahdhīb al-lugha* of Abū Manṣūr al-Azharī from Khurasan. So he achieved a knowledge of philology but rarely attained. He composed three odes full of rare expressions, as well as three letters—one in the style of Ibn al-'Amīd, one after the fashion of al-Ṣāḥib, and the third imitating al-Ṣābī ; then he ordered these to be bound, and the binding to be rubbed. So he suggested to the Amir that he should show this volume to Abū Manṣūr al-Jabbān, remarking that " we found this volume in the desert while hunting, and you must look it through and tell us what it contains ". Abū Manṣūr examined the book, and was baffled by many passages occurring in it. The Master suggested to him that " all you are ignorant of in this book you can find mentioned in such-and-such a context in the works on philology ", naming books well known in that science ; for he had memorized these phrases from them. Abū Manṣūr merely conjectured as to the words which the Master introduced, without any real certainty as to their meaning ; then he realized that the letters had really been composed by the Master, and that he had been induced to do so by the affront he had offered him that day ; he therefore extracted himself from the situation by apologizing to the Master. The latter then composed a work on philology which he entitled *Lisān al-'Arab* (" The Arab Language "), the like of which was never composed ; he did not transcribe it into a fair copy, so that at his death it was still in the rough draft and no man could discover a way to put it in order.

The Master had many remarkable experiences in the course of the various treatments he undertook, and he resolved to record them in the *Qānūn* ; he had actually annotated these on some quires, but they were lost before the *Qānūn* was completed. At Jurjan he had composed *al-Mukhtaṣar al-aṣghar* (" The Smaller Epitome ") on Logic, and it is this that he afterwards placed at the beginning of the *Najāt*. A copy of this came to Shiraz, where it was examined by a group of scholars ; they took objection to a number of points, and wrote their observations upon a separate quire. The Cadi of Shiraz was one of their persuasion, and he forwarded the quire to Abu 'l-Qāsim al-Kirmānī, the friend of Ibrāhīm ibn Bābā al-Dailamī, who had much to do with esoteric matters ; the Cadi enclosed a letter of his own to Abu 'l-Qāsim, and delivered the two documents into the hands of a post-messenger, with the request that he should present the quire to the Master and elicit from him his answers. Abu 'l-Qāsim came to the Master when the sun was yellowing upon a summer's day ; he showed him the letter and the quire ; the Master read the former and returned it to Abu 'l-Qāsim, while the latter he kept before him, examining it while a general conversation was in progress. Then Abu 'l-Qāsim went out ; and the Master commanded me to bring fair parchment and cut some quires. I sewed up five quires for

him, each of ten folios of a generous format. We prayed the
evening prayer ; candles were brought, and the Master ordered
drinks to be laid out. He made me and his brother sit with
him and drink, while he commenced to answer the questions
that had been propounded to him. So he continued writing and
drinking until half the night was gone, when I and his brother
were overcome by sleep ; he therefore bade us depart. In the
morning a knock came at the door, and there was the Master's
messenger summoning me. I found him at his prayers, and
before him the five quires completed. " Take them," he said,
" and go with them to Abu 'l-Qāsim al-Kirmānī ; tell him I
made haste to reply, so that the post-messenger might not be
delayed." When I brought the communication to him he was
most astonished ; he dispatched the messenger, and informed
his friends of the circumstances of the matter. The story
became quite an historic occasion.

While engaged upon his astronomical observations the Master
invented instruments the like of which had never been seen
before ; he also composed a treatise on the subject. I remained
eight years engaged upon this work, my object being to verify
the observations which Ptolemy reported on his own account,
and in fact some part of these were confirmed for me. The
Master also composed the *Kitāb al-Inṣāf* (" Book of Rectifica-
tion "), but on the day when Sultan Mas'ūd came to Isfahan
his army plundered the Master's luggage ; this book was part
of it, and was never seen again.

The Master was powerful in all his faculties, and he was
especially strong sexually ; this indeed was a prevailing passion
with him, and he indulged it to such an extent that his
constitution was affected ; yet he relied upon his powerful
constitution to pull him through. At last in the year when
'Alā' al-Daula fought Tāsh Farrāsh at the gates of al-Karkh,

the Master was attacked by the colic ; because of his eagerness
to cure himself—being afraid the Amir might suffer defeat, in
which case his sickness would not allow him to travel back—
he injected himself eight times in a single day, so that his intestines
were ulcerated and the abrasion showed on him. Yet he must
needs accompany 'Alā' al-Daula ; so they made haste towards
Idhaj, where the epilepsy which sometimes follows colic mani-
fested itself. Despite this he continued to treat himself, taking
injections for the abrasion and the rest of the colic. One day
he ordered the mixing of two *dangs* of celery-seed in the in-
jection, desiring to break the wind of the colic ; one of the
physicians attending him put in five *dirhams* of celery seed—
I know not whether purposely or in error, for I was not with
him—and the sharpness of the celery aggravated the abrasion.
He also took *mithradatum* for the epilepsy ; but one of his slaves
went and threw in a great quantity of opium, and he consumed
the mixture ; this being because they had robbed him of
much money from his treasury, and they desired to do away
with him so that they might escape the penalty of their
actions.

In this state the Master was brought to Isfahan, where he
continued to look after himself, though he was now so weak that
he could no longer stand ; nevertheless he went on treating
himself, until he was able to walk. He once more attended the
court of 'Alā' al-Daula ; however, he was incautious and indulged
his sexual appetite too far, so that he was never wholly cured,
suffering repeated relapses. Then 'Alā' al-Daula marched towards Hamadhan, and the Master went with him ; the same
malady revisited him upon the way, and when he finally reached
Hamadhan he knew that his strength was exhausted and no
longer adequate to repel the disease. He therefore gave up
treating himself, and took to saying, " The manager who used

to manage me is incapable of managing me any more ; so it is no use trying to cure my sickness."

So he continued some days, and was then transported to the Presence of his Lord. He was buried at Hamadhan, being 58 years old ; his death occurred in the year 428.

ON THE NATURE OF GOD

That there Is a Necessary Being

WHATEVER has being must either have a reason for its being, or have no reason for it. If it has a reason, then it is contingent, equally before it comes into being (if we make this mental hypothesis) and when it is in the state of being—for in the case of a thing whose being is contingent the mere fact of its entering upon being does not remove from it the contingent nature of its being. If on the other hand it has no reason for its being in any way whatsoever, then it is necessary in its being. This rule having been confirmed, I shall now proceed to prove that there is in being a being which has no reason for its being.

Such a being is either contingent or necessary. If it is necessary, then the point we sought to prove is established. If on the other hand it is contingent, that which is contingent cannot enter upon being except for some reason which sways the scales in favour of its being and against its not-being. If the reason is also contingent, there is then a chain of contingents linked one to the other, and there is no being at all ; for this being which is the subject of our hypothesis cannot enter into being so long as it is not preceded by an infinite succession of beings, which is absurd. Therefore contingent beings end in a Necessary Being.

Of the Unicity of God

It is not possible in any way that the Necessary Being should be two. Demonstration : Let us suppose that there is another necessary being : one must be distinguishable from the other, so that the terms " this " and " that " may be used with reference to them. This distinction must be either essential or accidental. If the distinction between them is accidental, this accidental element cannot but be present in each of them, or in one and not the other. If each of them has an accidental element by which it is distinguished from the other, both of them must be caused ; for an accident is what is adjoined to a thing after its essence is realized. If the accidental element is regarded as adhering to its being, and is present in one of the two and not in the other, then the one which has no accidental element is a necessary being and the other is not a necessary being. If, however, the distinction is essential, the element of essentiality is that whereby the essence as such subsists ; and if this element of essentiality is different in each and the two are distinguishable by virtue of it, then each of the two must be a compound ; and compounds are caused ; so that neither of them will be a necessary being. If the element of essentiality belongs to one only, and the other is one in every respect and there is no compounding of any kind in it, then the one which has no element of essentiality is a necessary being, and the other is not a necessary being. Since it is thus established that the Necessary Being cannot be two, but is All Truth, then by virtue of His Essential Reality, in respect of which He is a Truth, He is United and One, and no other shares with Him in that Unity : however the All-Truth attains existence, it is through Himself.

That God is Without Cause

A necessary being has no cause whatsoever. Causes are of four kinds : that from which a thing has being, or the active cause ; that on account of which a thing has being, or the final and completive cause ; that in which a thing has being, or the material cause ; and that through which a thing has being, or the formal cause.

The justification for limiting causes to these four varieties is that the reason for a thing is either internal in its subsistence, or a part of its being, or external to it.   If it is internal, then it is either that part in which the thing is, potentially and not actually, that is to say its matter ; or it is that part in which the thing becomes actually, that is to say its form.   If it is external, then it can only be either that from which the thing has being, that is to say the agent, or that on account of which the thing has being, that is to say its purpose and end.

Since it is established that these are the roots and principles of this matter, let us rest on them and clarify the problems which are constructed upon them.

Demonstration that He has no active cause : This is self-evident : for if He had any reason for being, this would be adventitious and that would be a necessary being.   Since it is established that He has no active cause, it follows on this line of reasoning that His Quiddity is not other than His Identity, that is to say, other than His Being ; neither will He be a subsistence or an accident.   There cannot be two, each of which derives its being from the other ; nor can He be a necessary being in one respect, and a contingent being in another respect.

Proof that His Quiddity is not other than His Identity, but rather that His Being is unified in His Reality : If His Being were not the same as His Reality, then His Being would be other than His Reality.   Every accident is caused, and every thing caused requires a reason.   Now this reason is either external to His Quiddity, or is itself His Quiddity : if it is external, then He is not a necessary being, and is not exempt from an active cause ; while if the reason is itself the Quiddity, then the reason must necessarily be itself a complete being in order that the being of another may result from it. Quiddity before being has no being ; and if it had being before this, it would not require a second being. The question therefore returns to the problem of being. If the Being of the Quiddity is accidental, whence did this Being supervene and adhere ? It is therefore established that the Identity of the Necessary Being is His Quiddity, and that He has no active cause ; the necessary nature of His Being is like the quiddity of all other things. From this it is evident that the Necessary Being does not resemble any other thing in any respect whatsoever ; for with all other things their being is other than their quiddity.

Proof that He is not an accident : An accident is a being in a locus. The locus is precedent to it, and its being is not possible without the locus. But we have stated that a being which is necessary has no reason for its being.

Proof that there cannot be two necessary beings, each deriving its being from the other : Each of them, in as much as it derives its being from the other, would be subsequent to the other, while at the same time by virtue of supplying being to the other, each would be precedent to the other : but one and the same thing cannot be both precedent and subsequent in relation to its being. Moreover, if we assume for the sake of argument that the other is non-existent : would the first then be a necessary being, or not ? If it were a necessary being, it would have no connexion with the other : if it were not a necessary being, it would be a contingent being and would require another necessary being. Since the Necessary Being is One, and does not derive Its being from any one, it follows that He is a Necessary Being in every respect ; while anything else derives its being from another.

Proof that He cannot be a Necessary Being in one respect and a contingent being in another respect : Such a being, in as much as it is a contingent being, would be connected in being with something else, and so it has a reason ; but in as much as it is a necessary being, it would have no connexions with anything else. In that case it would both have being and not have being ; and that is absurd.

Demonstration that He has no material and receptive cause : The receptive cause is the cause for the provision of the place in which a thing is received ; that is to say, the place prepared for the reception of being, or the perfection of being. Now the Necessary Being is a perfection in pure actuality, and is not impaired by any deficiency ; every perfection belongs to Him, derives from Him, and is preceded by His Essence, while every deficiency, even if it be metaphorical, is negated to Him. All perfection and all beauty are of His Being ; indeed, these are the vestiges of the perfection of His Being ; how then should He derive perfection from any other ? Since it is thus established that He has no receptive cause, it follows that He does not possess anything potentially, and that He has no attribute yet to be awaited ; on the contrary, His Perfection has been realized in actuality ; and He has no material cause. We say " realized in actuality ", using this as a common term of expression, meaning that every perfection belonging to any other is non-existent and yet to be awaited, whereas all perfection belonging to Him has being and is present. His Perfect Essence, preceding all relations, is One. From this it is manifest that His Attributes are not an augmentation of His Essence ; for if they were an augmentation of His Essence, the Attributes would be potential with reference to the Essence and the Essence would be the reason for the Attributes. In that case the Attributes would be subsequent to a precedent, so that they would be in one respect active and in another receptive ; their being active would be other than the aspect of their being receptive ; and in consequence they would possess two mutually exclusive aspects. Now this is impossible in the case of anything whatsoever ; when a body is in motion, the motivation is from one quarter and the movement from another.

If it were to be stated that His Attributes are not an augmentation of His Essence, but that they entered into the constitution of the Essence, and that the Essence cannot be conceived of as existing without these Attributes, then the Essence would be compound, and the Oneness would be destroyed. It is also evident, as a result of denying the existence of a receptive cause, that it is impossible for Him to change ; for the meaning of change is the passing away of one attribute and the establishment of another ; and if He were susceptible to change, He would possess potentially an element of passing-away and an element of establishment ; and that is absurd. It is clear from this that He has no opposite and no contrary ; for opposites are essences which succeed each other in the occupation of a single locus, there being between them the extreme of contrariety. But He is not receptive to accidents, much less to opposites. And if the term " opposite " is used to denote one who disputes with Him in His Rulership, it is clear too on this count that He has no opposite. It is further clear that it is impossible for Him not to be ; for since it is established that His Being is necessary, it follows that it is impossible for Him not to be ; because everything which exists potentially cannot exist actually, otherwise it would have two aspects. Anything which is receptive to a thing does not cease to be receptive when reception has actually taken place ; if this were not so, it would result in the removal of both being and not-being, and that is untenable. This rule applies to every essence and every unified reality, such as angels and human spirits ; they are not susceptible to not-being at all, since they are free from corporeal adjunctions.

Demonstration that He has no formal cause : A formal, corporeal cause only exists and is confirmed when a thing is possessed of matter : the matter has a share in the being of the form, in the same way that the form has a part in the disposition of the matter in being in actuality ; such a thing is therefore caused. It is further evident as a result of denying this cause to Him, that He is also to be denied all corporeal attributes, such as time, space, direction, and being in one place to the exclusion of all other ; in short, whatever is possible in relation to corporeal things is impossible in relation to Him.

Proof that He has no final cause : The final cause is that on account of which a thing has being ; and the First Truth has not being for the sake of anything, rather does everything exist on account of the perfection of His Essence, being consequent to His Being and derived from His Being. Moreover the final cause, even if it be posterior in respect of being to all other causes, yet it is mentally prior to them all. It is the final cause which makes the active cause become a cause in actuality, that is to say in respect of its being a final cause.

Since it is established that He is exalted above this last kind of cause too, it is clear that there is no cause to His Attributes. It is also evident that He is Pure Benevolence and True Perfection ; the meaning of His Self-Sufficiency likewise becomes manifest, namely that he approves of nothing and disapproves of nothing. For if He approved of anything, that thing would come into being and would continue to be ; while if He disapproved of anything, that thing would be converted into not-being and would be annulled. The very divergency of these beings proves the nullity of such a proposition ; for a thing which is one in every respect cannot approve of a thing and of its opposite. It is also not necessary for Him to observe the rule of greater expediency or of expediency, as certain

Qualitarians have idly pretended ; for if His acts of expediency were obligatory to Him, He would not merit gratitude and praise for such acts, since He would merely be fulfilling that which it is His obligation to perform, and He would be to all intents and purposes as one paying a debt ; He would therefore deserve nothing at all for such benevolence. In fact His acts proceed on the contrary from Him and for Him, as we shall demonstrate later.

His Attributes as Interpreted According to the Foregoing Principles

Since it is established that God is a Necessary Being, that He is One in every respect, that He is exalted above all causes, and that He has no reason of any kind for His Being ; since it is further established that His Attributes do not augment His Essence, and that He is qualified by the Attributes of Praise and Perfection ; it follows necessarily that we must state that He is Knowing, Living, Willing, Omnipotent, Speaking, Seeing, Hearing, and Possessed of all the other Loveliest Attributes. It is also necessary to recognize that His Attributes are to be classified as negative, positive, and a compound of the two : since His Attributes are of this order, it follows that their multiplicity does not destroy His Unity or contradict the necessary nature of His Being.   Pre-eternity for instance is essentially the negation of not-being in the first place, and the denial of causality and of primality in the second place ; similarly the term One means that He is indivisible in every respect, both verbally and actually. When it is stated that He is a Necessary Being, this means that He is a Being without a cause, and that He is the Cause of other than Himself : this is a combination of the negative and the positive. Examples of the positive Attributes are His being Creator, Originator, Shaper, and the entire Attributes of Action. As for the compound of both, this kind is illustrated by His being Willing and Omnipotent, for these Attributes are a compound of Knowledge with the addition of Creativeness.

God's Knowledge

God has knowledge of His Essence : His Knowledge, His Being Known and His Knowing are one and the same thing. He knows other than Himself, and all objects of knowledge. He knows all things by virtue of one knowledge, and in a single manner. His Knowledge does not change according to whether the thing known has being or not-being.

Proof that God has knowledge of His Essence : We have stated that God is One, and that He is exalted above all causes. The meaning of knowledge is the supervention of an idea divested of all corporeal coverings. Since it is established that He is One, and that He is divested of body, and His Attributes also ; and as this idea as just described supervenes upon Him ; and since whoever has an abstract idea supervening upon him is possessed of knowledge, and it is immaterial whether it is his essence or other than himself ; and as further His Essence is not absent from Himself ; it follows from all this that He knows Himself.

Proof that He is Knowledge, Knowing and Known : Knowledge is another term for an abstract idea. Since this idea is abstract, it follows that He is Knowledge ; since this abstract idea belongs to Him, is present with Him, and is not veiled from Him, it follows that He is Knowing ; and since this abstract idea does not supervene save through Him, it follows that He is Known. The terms employed in each case are different ; otherwise it might be said that Knowledge, Knowing and Known are, in relation to His Essence, one. Take your own experience as a parallel. If you know yourself, the object of your knowledge is either yourself or something else ; if the object of your knowledge is something other than yourself, then you do not know yourself. But if the object of your knowledge is yourself, then both the one knowing and the thing known are your self. If the image of your self is impressed upon your self, then it is your self which is the knowledge. Now if you look back upon yourself reflectively, you will not find any impression of the idea and quiddity of your self in yourself a second time, so as to give rise within you to a sense that your self is more than one. Therefore since it is established that He has intelligence of His Essence, and since His Intelligence is His Essence and does not augment His Essence, it follows that He is Knowing, Knowledge and Known without any multiplicity attaching to Him through these Attributes ; and there is no difference between " one who has knowledge " and " one who has intelligence ", since both are terms for describing the negation of matter absolutely.

Proof that He has knowledge of other than Himself : Whoever knows himself, if thereafter he does not know other than himself this is due to some impediment. If the impediment is essential, this implies necessarily that he does not know himself either ; while if the impediment is of an external nature, that which is external can be removed. Therefore it is possible— nay, necessary—that He should have knowledge of other than Himself, as you shall learn from this chapter.

Proof that He has knowledge of all objects of knowledge : Since it is established that He is a Necessary Being, that He is One, and that the universe is brought into being from Him and has resulted out of His Being ; since it is established further that He has knowledge of His Own Essence, His Knowledge of His Essence being what it is, namely that He is the Origin of all realities and of all things that have being ; it follows that nothing in heaven or earth is remote from His Knowledge

—on the contrary, all that comes into being does so by reason of Him : He is the causer of all reasons, and He knows that of which He is the Reason, the Giver of being and the Originator.

Proof that He knows all things by virtue of one knowledge, in a manner which changes not according to the change in the thing known : It has been established that His Knowledge does not augment His Essence, and that He is the Origin of all things that have being, while being exalted above accident and changes ; it therefore follows that He knows things in a manner unchanging. The objects of knowledge are a consequence of His Knowledge ; His Knowledge is not a consequence of the things known, that it should change as they change ; for His Knowledge of things is the reason for their having being. Hence it is manifest that Knowledge is itself Omnipotence. He knows all contingent things, even as He knows all things that have being, even though we know them not ; for the contingent, in relation to us, is a thing whose being is possible and whose not-being is also possible ; but in relation to Him one of the two alternatives is actually known. Therefore His Knowledge of genera, species, things with being, contingent things, manifest and secret things—this Knowledge is a single knowledge.

Acts Emanating from God

Since you now know that He is a Necessary Being, that He is One, and that He has no Attribute which augments His Essence (for that would imply a succession of various acts, whereas the Act of God is the vestiges of the Perfection of His Essence) ; this being so, it follows that His First Act is one. For if there had emanated from Him two acts, the emanation would have been in two different manners, for duality in the act implies duality in the agent. He who acts by virtue of his own essence, if his essence is one only one act emanates from it ; whereas if he has a duality of essence, he must be a compound ; and we have proved the impossibility of this as regards God. It follows necessarily that the first thing to emanate from God was not a body ; for every body is compounded of matter and form, and these require either two causes, or a single cause with two aspects ; this being so, it is impossible that these two should have emanated from God, it having been established that there is no compounding in God whatsoever. Since the first thing to emanate from God was not a body, it follows that it was an abstract substance, namely, the First Intelligence. This has been confirmed by the true religion, for the Prophet said, " The first thing God created was Intelligence," and again, " The first thing God created was the Pen." The phrase *Thou shalt not find any change in the Way of God* (Koran xxxiii. 62) refers to the perpetuity of the Creation ; the phrase *Thou shalt not find any alteration in the Way of God* (Koran xxxv. 41) refers to the perpetuity of the Command. Certainly, the Universe emanated from Him in due succession of order and media. So when we say that this Act emanated from Him through a reason, and that that reason was of Him also, this implies no imperfection in His Activity ; on the contrary, totality emanated from Him, through Him, and unto Him. Therefore all things having being emanated from Him according to a known order and known media : that which came later cannot be earlier, and that which came earlier cannot be later, for it is He Who causes things to be earlier and later. Indeed, the first thing having being that emanated from Him was the noblest ; thereafter came a descent from the nobler to the lower, until the lowliest of all was reached. First was Intelligence ; then Soul ; then the Body of Heaven ; then the materials of the four Elements with their forms (for their materials are common to all, only their forms differ). Then there is a mounting up from the lowliest to the noblest ;

the noblest of all ending at a degree parallel to the degree of the Intelligence. Through this process of origination and returning back, God is said to be the Originator and the Returner.

(From *al-Risālat al-'Arshīya.*)

PREDESTINATION

(AVICENNA was asked to explain the meaning of the Sufi saying, "To make known the secret of predestination is an act of heresy." His reply was as follows.)

This is an extremely recondite problem, and one which cannot be put on paper save in the language of cypher, a matter which may not be made known except as a hidden mystery : to disclose it in full would work much mischief to the people at large. The fundamental text in this connexion is the saying of the Prophet : " Predestination is the secret of God : do ye not disclose God's secret." It is related that a man asked the Caliph Ali about predestination, and he answered : " Predestination is a deep sea : do not embark upon it." Asked a second time, he replied : " It is a hard road : do not tread it." A third time asked, he retorted : " It is an arduous ascent : do not undertake it."

Now the secret of predestination is constructed upon certain propositions : first, the fact of an ordered universe, then the doctrine that men's actions will be rewarded and punished, and finally the belief that the soul will be restored after death.

First Proposition. There is nothing whatsoever in the entire world, and in all its higher and lower parts, which is excluded from the statement that God is the cause of its being and its origination in time, that God has knowledge of it and disposes it, and that God wills it to exist. On the contrary, the whole world is disposed and predetermined, known and willed by God ; though it is necessary to add that in describing the matter thus our intention is to describe it in terms confirmed as accurate

38

by the reason, not after the usage of scholastic theologians. Proofs and logical demonstrations can be offered in confirmation of this assertion. For if this world which we know were not compounded of the effects of good and evil forces, and of the products of both righteousness and corruption in its inhabitants, the world order would not have been fulfilled completely. If only pure righteousness prevailed in the world, this world would not be the world we know, but another world. But since it was necessary that the world should be compounded after this manner and order, it follows that both righteousness and corruption prevail in it.

Second Proposition. The ancient philosophers held that " reward " is the supervening of a certain pleasure in the soul according to the degree to which it achieves perfection, while " punishment " is the supervening of a certain pain in the soul according to the degree to which it remains imperfect. The continuance of the soul in a state of imperfection is the state of remoteness from God : that is what is meant by being under a curse, suffering punishment, encountering Divine Wrath and Anger : the pain which the soul has to endure is a consequence of that imperfection. Similarly the perfection of the soul is what is meant by saying that God is pleased with it, that it is near and nigh unto God and close to God's Presence. Such then is the meaning of reward and punishment : this and nothing else.

Third Proposition. Restoration after death is the return of human souls to their own world : therefore God said, *O soul at rest within thyself, return to thy Lord, well pleased and well pleasing* (Koran lxxxix. 27). These summary statements require of course to be supported by logical demonstrations.

These propositions being established as valid, it is necessary for us to add that the apparent evils which occur in this world cannot be accepted by the judgment of reason as what is purposed of the world : good only is purposed : evil is annihilation.

Plato held that the whole was purposed and willed ; and that the commandments and prohibitions relating to the acts of responsible beings in the world are to be understood as encouragements for those of whom it is known in God's fore-knowledge that they will perform the things so commanded, and deterrents to those of whom it is known in God's fore-knowledge that they will refrain from the things so forbidden. The commandment is a cause of the act happening in the case of those of whom it is known that the act will occur from them ; the prohibition is the cause of abstention in those who are repelled from the wickedness for that reason. But for the commandment, the agent of good would not be encouraged to act ; but for the prohibition there would not be this abstention on his part. Plato imagined that it would have been possible for corruption to occur a hundred per cent but for this pro-hibition ; with the intervention of the prohibition, it has only occurred fifty per cent. In the same way if there had been no commandment, nothing of righteousness would have occurred at all ; with the supervening of the commandment fifty per cent of righteousness resulted.

As for praise and blame, these have two objects : one, to incite the agent of good to repeat the like act which it is willed should occur from him ; the other, to deter the one from whom the act has resulted from repeating a like act, and to ensure that the one from whom such an act may result may abstain from doing what it is willed should not occur from him, it being within his competence to do that thing.

It is not right to hold that reward and punishment are in accordance with what the scholastic theologians suppose—to acquit the fornicator, for example, by loading him with chains and shackles, to burn him with fire again and again, and to loose snakes and scorpions against him. Such conduct is the way of those who desire to have their revenge on their enemy, by some mischief or pain befalling him as a reprisal for his aggression against them ; and it is clearly untenable that God should be possessed of such an attribute, or that He should so visit one whom He willed to refrain from committing a like action, or to be restrained from repeating such a deed. It is likewise not to be conceived, as they have imagined, that after the resurrection any soul shall again be made responsible, or be made the object of any commandment or prohibition, so that it should be restrained or refrain from a course of action by reason of being a spectator of Divine reward and punishment in that world.

As for the sanctions established by the sacred law with reference to those who commit acts of disobedience against God, these operate after the same fashion as the prohibition itself, in that they restrain those who will abstain from such an act, whereas but for the prohibition it is conceivable that that act might occur from them. There is also some advantage in having sanctions, since they prevent the offender from entering upon a further course of corruption. Moreover men must be bound by one kind of fetter or another—either of the sacred law, or of reason —in order that the order of the world may be maintained in full perfection : it is a matter of common observation, that if any man were loosed from both sets of chains the corruption he would commit would be quite intolerable, and the entire order of the world's affairs would be impaired as a result of his release from both kinds of fetters. But God knows better, and is wiser.

Now it is well known that man differs from all other animals in that he cannot enjoy a good life in isolation and alone, managing all his affairs without any partner to assist him in the fulfil- ment of his needs. A man must perforce attain satisfaction by means of another of his species, whose needs in turn are satisfied by him and his like : thus, one man will act as conveyor, another as baker, another as tailor, another as sewer ; when all unite together, the needs of all are satisfied. For this reason they were constrained to construct cities and societies. Those makers of cities who did not observe the conditions required in their undertaking, confining themselves only to coming together in one community, achieved a kind of life little resembling that which is proper to men, being devoid of those ' perfections ' which men require.

This being so, it is necessary for men both to associate with each other, and to behave like citizens. This is obvious ; it also follows that it is necessary to the life and survival of mankind that there should be co-operation between them, which can only be realized through a common transaction of business ; in addition to all the other means which secure the same purpose. This transaction requires a code of law and just regulation, which is their turn call for a lawgiver and regulator. Such a man must be in the position to speak to men, and to constrain them to accept the code ; he must therefore be a man.

Now it is not feasible that men should be left to their own opinions in this matter so that they will differ each from the other, every man considering as justice that which favours him, and as injustice that which works against his advantage. The survival and complete self-realization of the human race requires the existence of such a lawgiver, far more than for instance the growth of hair on the eyelashes and eyebrows, the development of a hollow instep, and such other advantages as are not necessary to survival but are at the most merely useful to that end.

It is entirely possible for a righteous man to exist ; and it is not feasible that the Divine Providence should have required the other small advantages, and not have required this which is the foundation of them all ; neither is it reasonable to suppose that the First Principle and the Angels should have been aware of the former and not have known of the latter. Finally it is not likely that this, being a matter known to be existentially possible and actually necessary to establish a beneficent order, should yet not exist ; indeed, how should it not exist, seeing that that which depends and is constructed upon its existence does in fact already exist ?

It follows therefore that there should exist a prophet, and that he should be a man ; it also follows that he should have some distinguishing feature which does not belong to other men, so that his fellows may recognise him as possessing something which is not theirs, and so that he may stand out apart from them. This distinguishing feature is the power to work miracles.

Such a man, if and when he exists, must prescribe laws for mankind governing all their affairs, in accordance with God's ordinance and authority, God inspiring him and sending down the Holy Spirit upon him. The fundamental principle upon which his code rests will be to teach them that they have One Creator, Almighty and Omniscient, Whose commandment must of right be obeyed ; that the Command must belong to Him Who possesses the power to create ; and that He has prepared for those who obey Him a future life of bliss, but wretchedness

D

for such as disobey Him.   So the masses will receive the prescriptions, sent down upon his tongue from God and the Angels,
with heedful obedience.

It is not necessary for him to trouble their minds with any
part of the knowledge of God, save the knowledge that He is
One, True, and has no like ; as for going beyond this doctrine,
so as to charge them to believe in God's existence as not to be
defined spatially or verbally divisible, as being neither without
the world nor within it, or anything of that sort—to do this
would impose a great strain upon them and would confuse
the religious system which they follow already, bringing them
to a pass wherefrom only those rare souls can escape who enjoy
especial favour, and they exceedingly uncommon.   The gener-
ality of mankind cannot imagine these things as they really are
except by hard toil ; few indeed are they who can conceive
the truth of this Divine Unity and Sublimity.   The rest are
soon apt to disbelieve in this sort of Being, or they fall down
upon the road and go off into discussions and speculations which
prevent them from attending to their bodily acts, and often
enough cause them to fall into opinions contrary to the good of
society and inconsistent with the requirements of truth.   In
such circumstances their doubts and difficulties would multiply,
and it would be hard indeed by words to control them : not
every man is ready to understand metaphysics, and in any case
it would not be proper for any man to disclose that he is in
possession of a truth which he conceals from the masses ; indeed,
he must not allow himself so much as to hint at any such thing.
His duty is to teach men to know the Majesty and Might of
God by means of symbols and parables drawn from things which
they regard as mighty and majestic, imparting to them simply
this much, that God has no equal, no like and no partner.

Similarly he must establish in them the belief in an afterlife, in a manner that comes within the range of their imagination and will be satisfying to their souls ; he will liken the happiness and misery there to be experienced in terms which they can understand and conceive. As for the truth of these matters, he will only adumbrate it to them very briefly, saying that it is something which " eye hath not seen nor ear heard ", and that there is pleasure awaiting us beyond the grave which is a mighty kingdom, or pain that is an abiding torment. God certainly knows the beneficent aspect of all this, and it is always right to take what God knows exactly for what it implies. There is therefore no harm in his discourse being interspersed with sundry hints and allusions, to attract those naturally qualified for specula-tion to undertake philosophical research into the nature of religious observances and their utility in terms of this world and the next.

Now this person, the prophet, is not of the kind that often comes into the world, in every age : the gross matter able to receive his sort of ' perfection ' occurs in but few temperaments. It follows from this that the prophet must devise means of securing the survival of his code and laws in all the spheres of human welfare. There is no doubt that the advantage in this is, that men will continue to be aware of the existence of God and of an afterlife ; and the danger of their forgetting these things, a generation after the prophet's mission, will be circum-vented. He must therefore prescribe certain acts which men should repeat at close intervals, so that if the time for the per-formance of one act is missed there may soon be an opportunity for performing the next like act while the memory is still fresh and has not yet become obliterated.

These acts must of course be linked up with some means of calling God and the afterlife to mind, else they will be useless : this mnemonic can only consist of set words to be uttered, or set resolves to be intended in the imagination. Men must also be told that these acts are means of winning God's favour and of qualifying for a great and generous reward : these acts should in fact be of such a sort, and should be like the religious observances prescribed for men to follow. In a word, these acts should be reminders ; and those reminders must be either certain motions, or the denial of certain motions resulting in other motions. The former category may be illustrated by the instance of formal prayers, the latter by fasting ; for though fasting is in itself a negative idea, it stirs nature violently and so reminds the faster that what he is doing is not meaningless, with the result that he remembers what his intention is in fasting, namely to win the favour of Almighty God.

He should also if possible mix in with these observances other interests, in order to strengthen and extend the code, and to make their practice generally advantageous in a material sense also. Examples of this are Jehad and Pilgrimage. He should specify certain places in the world as the most suitable for worship, stating that they belong exclusively to God ; certain obligatory acts must also be specified as being done for God's sake only—as for instance the offering of sacrifices, which are of great help in this connexion. The place which is advantageous in this context, if it be the town where the lawgiver took refuge and dwelt, will also serve the purpose of bringing him to mind, an advantage second only to that of remembering God and the Angels. This single place of refuge cannot be close at hand for the whole community of the Faith ; obviously therefore it must be prescribed as a place for migration, and for journeying unto.

The noblest of these observances from a certain point of view is that one in which the performer assumes that he is addressing God in private converse, that he is turning to God and standing before Him. This observance is Prayer. Certain steps preparatory to prayer must also be prescribed, similar to those which a man customarily undertakes of his own accord before entering the presence of a human ruler ; namely, purification and cleansing. The regulations laid down for these should be effective and impressive. The act of prayer should further be accompanied by those attitudes and rules of conduct usually observed in the presence of kings : humility, quietness, lowering the eyes, keeping the hands and feet withdrawn, not turning about and fidgeting. For every moment of the act of worship, appropriate and seemly rules and usages should be prescribed. All these conditions of religious observance serve the useful purpose of keeping the people's thoughts fixed firmly upon the recollection of God ; in this way they will continue in their close attachment to the laws and ordinances of the Faith ; without these reminders they will be apt to forget all about it one or two generations after the prophet's death. These practices will also be of enormous advantage to them in the hereafter, by purifying and lifting up their souls as we have already shown.

So far as the elect are concerned, the advantage they derive from all these prescriptions is mainly connected with the afterlife. We have established above the true nature of the hereafter, and proved that happiness in the world to come is to be acquired by cleansing and uplifting the soul, through removing it far from such bodily conditions as conflict with the means of securing that happiness. Spiritual elevation is achieved through the acquisition of moral qualities and virtuous habits, which in their turn are acquired by means of acts calculated to divert the soul from the body and the senses and to remind it of its true substance.

If the soul is frequently turned in towards itself, it will not be affected by the physical circumstances of the body. It will

be reminded and helped to do this by acts which are in themselves fatiguing, and outside the usual habit of the reason;
indeed, the reason itself is stimulated by them to undertake these
tasks.   They fatigue the body and the animal faculties, destroy-
ing their inclination to take things easily, to be slothful and
unwilling to go to any trouble, to dull the natural zest and
avoid all discipline save for the purpose of getting advantages
in the form of bestial pleasures.   The soul will be constrained
to attempt these motions by the very recollection of God, of
the Angels and of the world of perfect happiness, whether it
will or no;   consequently it will become firmly disposed to
chafe at the influences of the body and will acquire the habit
of dominating it and not to be merely passive in its control.
Bodily actions as they occur will not then affect the soul so
powerfully and habitually as would be the case if the soul were
satisfied and content to submit to the body in everything.   All
this proves the truth of the saying, that good habits drive out
evil ones.   If a man continues in this course, he will acquire
the habit of turning automatically towards the true, and away
from the false;   he will become thoroughly prepared and ready
to be delivered into celestial happiness when the body is left
behind.

If a man performs these acts without believing them to be
a duty imposed by God, and in spite of this his each act is accompanied by the remembrance of God, and a turning away from
all other things, he will be worthy to acquire some measure
of this spiritual fervour: how much the more, then, if he
follows this use knowing that the Prophet has come from God
and has been sent to men by God, that it was metaphysically
necessary that he should be sent, and that all the laws which
he established were those which he was obliged by God to
prescribe, he acting in all this as God's agent.   For the Prophet

was truly charged by God to impose these religious observances
upon his followers : observances which are of benefit to men
in that they perpetuate among them the Prophet's laws and
ordinances, which are the means whereby they live at all, and
by stimulating them to spiritual zeal bring them near to the
nigh Presence of God in the world to come.

Such a man is richly qualified to dispose the affairs of his
fellows in a manner securing the regular provision of their well-
being in this world, and their ultimate salvation in the world
to come : he is a man distinguished above all his fellows by
his godliness.

(From the *Kitāb al-Najāt*.)

ON PRAYER

On the Nature of Prayer

WHEN God had created the animals, after the plants, the minerals and the elements, and after the spheres, the stars, the unsubstantial spirits and the intelligences perfect in themselves ; when He had completed His work of origination and creation, He desired to finish His creation with the most perfect species, even as He had begun it with the most perfect genus. He therefore distinguished Man from out of all His creatures, so that as the beginning had been with Intelligence, so too the conclusion should be. He began with the noblest of substances, Intelligence, and He concluded with the noblest of beings, the Intelligent. The high purpose of creation was Man, and nothing else.

Having realized all this, thou must know that Man is the Microcosm ; and as all other beings are graded in their world, so too man is graded according to his deeds and his nobility. Some men there are whose deeds accord with those of angels ; some whose acts accord with those of devils, so that they perish. For Man has not been produced out of one thing only, that he should be subject to a single set of conditions : God has compounded him of many things of various sorts, and temperaments of divers kinds. God divided Man's substantiality into body and soul, the former containing his grosser and the latter his subtler elements. He bestowed upon him sense and reason, both secret and manifest ; then He adorned his outward and manifest part, his body, with the five senses in the amplest degree and fullest order. Next out of his inward and secret parts He chose those which were strongest and noblest. The physical element He implanted in his liver, to regulate his digestion and evacuation (or attraction and repulsion), to balance the members and replace by means of nourishment the parts lost through dissolution. The animal element He associated with his heart, connected with the faculties of appetite and anger, to accord with the congenial and oppose the uncongenial : this He made the fountainhead of the five senses, and the source of the imagination and of movement. Lastly He fashioned the human, rational soul in the brain, which He lodged in the highest situation and most appropriate station. He adorned it with thought, memory and recollection, and gave the intellectual substance power over it, that it might be as it were a commander with the faculties for soldiers ; the " common-sense " served as a courier, to act as an intermediary between the brain and the senses. The senses were to be the spies of the brain, each stationed at its appropriate gate, to sally forth from time to time into their own world and pick up all that was let fall by their fellows, which they should convey to the particular messenger ; the latter would then deliver it, sealed and enveloped, to the faculty of the intelligence, to discriminate and choose what accorded with it, and to reject that which was not genuine.

Man was thus equipped with these souls out of all the world, through each faculty sharing with one class or other of living beings. By virtue of the animal soul he shares with the animals ; his physical soul links him with the plants ; his human soul is a bond between him and the angels. Moreover each of these faculties has a special sphere, and a particular function to perform : according as one of the three prevails over the other two, the individual is defined by that prevalent sphere, and related after his perception to his own genus. Similarly each function has its own sphere, its own reward, and its own purpose.

The function of the physical soul is to eat and drink, to

maintain the parts of the body, and to cleanse the body of
superfluities : that is all : it has no business to compete or dispute with the function of any other. The purpose of its function
is to keep the body in order and the limbs in proper balance,
while supplying strength to the physique. The proper order
of the body is proved by a well-oiled flesh, sturdy limbs and
a strong physique ; and these are acquired from eating and
drinking. The reward of the physical soul's function is not
to be expected in the spiritual world, and does not wait upon
the resurrection, for this soul will not be raised up after death :
it resembles a plant, in that when it dies it is dispersed and
obliterated, never to be recalled to life.

The function of the animal soul is movement, imagination,
and the defence of all the body by good management. Its
necessary sphere and particular function is confined to appetite
and anger ; anger is a branch of appetite, since it seeks to repress,
to overcome, to dominate and to tyrannize ; these are the
various sorts of leadership, and leadership is the fruit of appetite.
The special function of the animal soul is fundamentally appetite,
and incidentally anger. Its purpose is to preserve the body
through the faculty of anger, and to perpetuate the species
through the faculty of appetite ; for the species is perpetuated
always by means of generation, and generation is regulated by
the faculty of appetite ; while the body remains guarded from
injuries by virtue of its being defended, which means to dominate
the enemy, to bar the gate of harm, and to prevent the harmful
effects of tyranny, and all these ideas are contained and confined
within the faculty of anger. Its reward is the realization of its
hopes in this lower world ; it is not to be expected after death,
for the animal soul dies with the body, and will not be raised
up at the resurrection. It resembles all the animals, in that it
is not qualified to receive the Divine Allocution, and may not

therefore expect any reward. When the emanation of a thing is annihilated, it cannot be raised up after death ; upon death its entire existence dies, and its happiness is past.

The function of the human, rational soul is the noblest function of all, for it is itself the noblest of spirits. Its function consists of reflecting upon things of art and meditating upon things of beauty : its gaze being turned towards the higher world, it loves not this lower abode and meaner station. Belonging as it does to the higher side of life and to the primal substances, it is not its business to eat and drink, neither does it require luxury and coition ; rather its function is to wait for the revelation of truths, and to reflect with perfect intuition and unclouded wit upon the perception of subtle ideas, reading with the eye of inner vision the tablet of Divine Mystery and opposing with strenuous devices the causes of vain fancy. It is distinguished from other spirits by the possession of perfect reason and far-reaching, all-embracing thought ; its ambition and striving all through life is to purify the sensual impressions and to perceive the world of intelligible truths. God has singled it out above all other spirits for the gift of the faculty of reason. Reasoning is the tongue of the angels, who have no speech or utterance ; reasoning belongs to them especially, which is perception without sensing and communication without words. Man's relation to the world of Spirit is established by reasoning ; speech follows after it. If a man possesses no knowledge of reasoning, he is incapable of expressing truth.

The function of the soul is therefore as we have summarized it here, in the fewest possible words. The subject can be greatly amplified, but we have abbreviated its discussion here, since our purpose in this treatise is not to give an account of the human faculties and their functions. We have therefore brought forward and established merely what we required by way of preface.

The function peculiar to the human soul is knowledge and perception : its use is manifold. To it belong remembrance, humble petition, and worship. When a man knows his Lord by the medium of his thoughts, and apprehends His Essence through his reason acting upon his knowledge, and perceives His Goodness with his intellect acting upon his reason, he considers attentively the inward nature of creation, and perceives creation as most perfectly displayed in the heavenly bodies and supernal substances : these are the most perfect of created beings because they are the furthest removed from corruption, impurities and diverse compounds. Then he sees within his rational soul a semblance of that immortality and rationality which subsist in those bodies. Reflecting upon the Creator, he realizes that Command is indeed associated with Creation, as God Himself declares : *To Him belong the Creation and the Command* (Koran vii. 52). Knowing thus that the Divine Emanation descends into creation out of the world of Command (which is to say, those spiritual substances), he desires ardently to comprehend their several ranks, and is eager to establish relations with them and to resemble their elevation. So he is ever humbling himself and meditating passionately, with prayers and fasting ; and he attains to a great reward. For the human soul has indeed a reward : it survives after the body has perished, and decays not with the lapse of time ; it is raised up after death. Death is the separation of the soul from the body ; resurrection is its union with those spiritual substances ; the soul's reward and felicity come after these events. A man is rewarded according to his acts ; if he is perfect in works, he obtains an ample reward ; but if his acts are imperfect and fall short, in like measure is his felicity imperfect and his reward falls short, so that he remains forever sorrowful and downcast, nay, forsaken and damned. If his animal and physical faculties prevail over his rational faculty, he is bewildered after death and wretched after resurrection ; but if his blameworthy faculties are deficient, and his soul is divorced from evil thoughts and mean passions, if his self is adorned with the ornament of reason and the necklace of knowledge, if he has trained himself to acquire all praiseworthy qualities, he will remain forever pure, refined and happy ; having attained his heavenly reward, he will abide eternally with his own dear kith and kin.

Now that we have finished this preamble, we would remark that it is prayer which causes the human, rational soul to resemble the heavenly bodies, eternally worshipping Absolute Truth, and seeking the imperishable reward. The Prophet of God declared, " Prayer is the foundation-stone of religion " ; and religion is the purifying of the human soul of all devilish impurities and carnal suggestions, turned away from mean worldly interests. Prayer is the worship of the First Cause, the One Supreme and Mightiest Worshipful ; adoration is to know Him Whose Being is Necessary. It needs not that we should interpret the text *And jinns and men were not created save to worship Me* (Koran li. 56) as meaning " to know Me ", for worship is knowledge, and to be aware of the existence of One Whose Being is necessary and absolute, being seized of His Being with a pure heart, a spirit undefiled, and a soul wholly devoted to Him. The real nature of prayer is therefore to know Almighty God in His Uniqueness, as a Being wholly Necessary, Whose Essence is infinitely exalted and Whose Qualities are infinitely holy, with habits of sincerity in prayer ; by which sincerity I mean, that one should know the Qualities of God in such a manner that there remains no opening to a multiplicity of gods, no intent to join others to His worship. Whoso acts thus may be said to be truly sincere in prayer, not erring or straying from the path ; but he who acts not thus is a forger, a liar and a rebel against God, Who is Supreme and Omnipotent beyond all such confoundings.

Of the Outward Form and Inward Truth of Prayer

When thou hast understood all that we have already stated in this discourse regarding the nature of prayer, it now becomes necessary for thee to realize that prayer is divided into two parts, one being outward (the part of discipline, that appertains to the body) and one inward (the real prayer, that concerns the soul). The outward part of prayer is that prescribed by the religious law and recognized as a fundamental duty of religion : our Lawgiver imposed it as an obligation for every man, calling it *ṣalāt* and making it the foundation of faith, saying, " There is no faith in him who has no *ṣalāt*, and there is no faith in him who is not faithful."

The numbers of prayer are recognized, and its times precisely laid down : the Prophet counted it as the noblest of devotions, and assigned it the highest rank among all acts of worship. This outward or disciplinary part is connected with the body, because it is composed of certain postures and elements such as recitation, genuflection and prostration : while the body is likewise compounded of certain principles and elements, such as water, earth, air, fire and similar temperaments. The body is the physical envelope of man ; and that which is composed is itself connected with its like. These postures of prayer, composed of recitation, genuflection and prostration and occurring in regular and definite numbers, are visible evidence of that real prayer which is connected with and adherent to the rational soul. They act as controlling the body, to bring it into tune with the general harmony of the universe. The numbers of prayer are part of the scheme of discipline prescribed by the religious law ; the Lawgiver imposed them upon every adult man of sound mind. In this manner the body is made to imitate that attitude, proper to the soul, of submission to the Higher Self, so that through this act man may be distinguished from the beasts. The beasts are not favoured by the Divine Allocution ; they are exempt from Judgment ; they do not look for Divine chastisement and reward. Man however has received the Word of God, and shall be chastised or rewarded according as he obeys the commandments and prohibitions of religion and reason. The Law follows in the wake of Reason. The Lawgiver, having observed that Reason imposes upon the rational soul the duty of prayer true and unadulterated—the knowledge and apprehension of God—therefore prescribed prayer for the body as an outward symbol of that other prayer ; he compounded it of numbers, and arranged it precisely in the most beautiful forms and most perfect postures, so that the body might follow after the spirit in worship, even though it does not accord with it in rank. The Lawgiver realized that all men are not capable of mounting the steps of reason ; they therefore required some regular bodily training and discipline to oppose their natural inclinations. He pioneered a road and fashioned a rule consisting of these numbers of prayer, which men could generally follow and understand with the senses ; they would be connected with the outer parts of man, and would prevent him from imitating the beasts and other animals. He ordained this as a supreme commandment, saying, " Pray in the manner that ye have seen me pray." There is much advantage in this, and a general benefit which will not escape the notice of any intelligent man, even though the ignorant may not acknowledge the fact.

As for the second or inward part or truth of prayer : this is to contemplate God with a pure heart, and a spirit abstracted and cleansed of all desires. This part does not follow the way of bodily numbers and sensual elements, but rather the path of pure thoughts and eternal spirits. The Prophet himself was often preoccupied with the true apprehension of God, and was thereby prevented from following the numerical order of formal prayer, which he sometimes shortened and sometimes prolonged. This is the kind of prayer that is exclusively the concern of the intellect ; reason confirms this statement, bearing in mind the Prophet's words, " The man at prayer is in secret converse with his Lord." It is obvious to the intelligent man that such converse is not effected through the physical parts and the audible and visible tongue, because conversation and converse of that kind can only take place with somebody contained in space and determined by time. As for the One Supreme Being, Who is circumscribed not by space nor touched by time, to Whom reference cannot be made through any direction, Whose Predicament varies not in respect of any particular Attribute, and Whose Essence changes not at any time : how should He be perceived by man, who is limited by form and body, is subject to physical dimensions and empowered only to the extent of his senses, faculties and physical frame ? How should mortals have converse with Him, the confines of Whose Directions they know not, neither perceive the environs of the paths of His Tendings ? The True and Absolute Being is absent from the sensible world, and is neither seen nor contained in space ; while it is the wont of corporeal beings only to have converse and concourse with such beings as they can see and point to, reckoning as absent and far off any that they cannot so behold ; and converse with one absent is plainly impossible. It is axiomatic that He Whose Being is Necessary must be absent and far off from these physical bodies, since they are subject to accidental change and corporeal accident, require space and preservation, and by virtue of their weight and grossness dwell upon the face of this dark earth. Even those simple, sublime substances which are not touched by time, nor set in any measured space, flee away from these bodies as animated by the hostility of contrariety ; and the Necessary Being is loftier than all simple substances, far more exalted and sublime than they—how then should He be associated with by sensual, corporeal beings ?

Since it is established that it is impossible and absurd to assert and specify God in relation to any direction, it is obviously still more absurd to suppose or conjecture that converse with Him may be established through the external senses. The Prophet's words, " The man at prayer is in secret converse with his Lord," are therefore only to be predicated of that inward knowledge which belongs solely to pure souls that are abstracted and free from events in time and directions in space : they contemplate God intellectually, and behold Him with spiritual, not corporeal vision. It is thus evident that true prayer is spiritual contemplation, and that pure worship is spiritual Divine love.

All the foregoing argument proves conclusively that prayer is of two kinds. And now we would observe that the outward, disciplinary part of prayer, which is connected with personal motions according to certain numbered postures and confined elements, is an act of abasement, and of passionate yearning on the part of this lower, partial, compound and limited body towards the lunary sphere ; which latter, operating through the Active Intellect, controls this world of generation and decay. Praying after this fashion is converse with that Intellect by means of the human tongue ; for it sustains and controls all created beings. Outward prayer is a humble petition that the Active Intellect may preserve and maintain the integrity of the person so abasing himself in worship and emulation, that he shall thereby continue guarded and protected against the misfortunes

E

of time, so long as he remains in this world.   The true, inward part of prayer, which is unassociated with postures and divorced from all changes, is an abasement unto God through the rational soul, which knows and is aware of the Unicity of the True God : this kind of prayer has no reference to any direction, and is not in any way confounded with any physical element.   It is an imploring of Absolute Being to perfect the soul through contemplation of Him, and to complete the worshipper's felicity through the inner knowledge and apprehension of Him.   The Intellectual Command and Holy Emanation descends from the Heavenly Void into the confines of the rational soul as a result of this prayer ;   this form of worship is imposed without corporeal weariness or human imposition.   Whoso prays after this fashion is delivered out of his physical faculties and natural vestiges, and climbs the intellectual steps until he beholds the mysteries of Eternity.   It is to this that God refers in the words, *Prayer prohibits abomination and all blameworthy acts ;   the remembrance of God is greater than all other deeds ;   and God knoweth what things ye do* (Koran xxix. 44).

What Part of Prayer is Incumbent upon Whom

Now that we have set forth the nature of prayer, and shown that it is divided into two parts each of which we have explained, it remains for us to remark to which class of people each part belongs and is appropriate.

It is clear that man has in him something of the lower world and something of the upper world also : these two portions of human nature we have briefly expounded above. It has emerged from the discussion that prayer is divided into the disciplinary-physical and the real-spiritual ; I have accorded each part sufficient treatment as befits the scope of the present treatise. I will now add that men vary one from the other according to the influence of the powers of the spirits compounded in each. If the physical and animal element prevails, he will be passionately attached to the body, loving to keep it in good order, nurtured and healthy, fond of feeding it, giving it to drink and clothing it, attentive to securing its advantage and to ward off mischief from it.   A man so intending is to be numbered among the animals, nay, he is to be counted as belonging to the order of the brute beasts ; his days are wholly absorbed in caring for his bodily welfare ; his every moment is dedicated to his personal interests ; he is heedless of the Creator and ignorant of the True God.   It is therefore not permissible for him to neglect the commandment of the religious law, which is absolutely binding and incumbent upon him.   If he is not accustomed to perform this duty, he must be disciplined and compelled to such a point that he will not omit to discharge his obligation, to be reverent and yearningly to betake himself to the Active Intellect and the Revolving Sphere, that it may emanate in its bounty over him and deliver him from the chastisement inherent in his existence, freeing him from bodily desires and bringing him safely to the true goal of his hopes.   And truly, if but a little portion of the emanation of that grace were denied to him, swiftly would he hasten into great evil, and become the lowest of the animals and ravening beasts.

As for the man in whom the spiritual faculties prevail, so that his rational faculty dominates his passion, and his soul is abstracted from terrestrial preoccupations and the attachments of this lower world : such a man has attained true security and spiritual worship ; and that pure prayer which we have described is incumbent upon him most urgently and is his most strong obligation.   Being ready in the cleanliness of his soul to receive the emanation of God's grace, if he but turns towards God in love and is earnest to worship Him, supernal blessings and heavenly felicity will swiftly flow over him ; when the time comes for him to be separated from the body and to depart out of this life, he will immediately contemplate his God, dwelling in His Presence and enjoying the company of those his true kin, the dwellers in the Divine Kingdom, the bodies of the celestial worlds.

This is the type of prayer which was incumbent upon our Lord and Founder of our Faith, Muhammad the Elect of God, on the night when he was separated from his body and divested of all worldly desire, so that there remained with him no trace of animal passion or the pull of natural wants. He enjoyed converse with God in his soul and intellect, saying, " O Lord, I have discovered a strange joy this night : grant me the means to perpetuate it, and provide for me a way that will always bring me unto it." It was then that God commanded the Prophet to pray, saying, " O Muhammad, the man at prayer is in secret converse with his Lord."

Those who practise only the outer part of prayer experience but a defective portion of that joy ; but those who pray in the spirit know that joy in full and abundant measure ; and the fuller that measure is, the ampler is their reward.

This is as much as I desired to say briefly in the present treatise, and only then after hesitating long to embark at all upon the interpretation of prayer, the dissecting of its real nature and the setting forth of its two parts. But when I saw intelligent men disregarding its external forms, without considering its inward meanings, I felt that it was my duty to explain the subject, and my obligation to state these facts. The intelligent man will thus be able to reflect upon what I have said, and the learned and fully qualified man proceed to examine the matter further ; he will then come to realize who is called upon to discharge the disciplinary part of prayer only, and to whom the spiritual side is appropriate and attainable. He will find it easy to proceed along the path of worship, and to persist in his prayers ; enjoying converse with God, not indeed as in person, by word of mouth, by ocular vision and the senses, but in the spirit and reason, with the inward vision and speculative insight ; for it is a delusion to suppose that one can ever approach God in person, and a vain fancy to desire to see Him, and to worship and converse with Him through the senses.

All the other ordinances of religion are explicable along the lines which have been sketched in the present treatise. We would have desired to expound each particular act of worship separately ; but it was impossible for us to enter upon matters which may not fitly be communicated to every man. We have accordingly established this clear and straightforward division, knowing that a mere hint is sufficient for the liberal mind. And I forbid that this treatise be presented to any man whom passion has led astray, or whose heart has been stamped with its brand. The impotent man can have no conception of the pleasures of intercourse, any more than the blind man can believe the joys of sight.

I wrote this treatise, thanks be to God's assistance and abundant grace, in a period of less than half an hour, and that despite numerous hindrances and little leisure. I therefore ask the indulgence of those who read it ; and I request that all who are blessed with the emanation of reason, and the light of justice, will not disclose my secret, even though they may be secure from any mischief that I may be the cause of. The matter rests with my Creator ; and my Creator knows all my affair, and none other beside Him.

THE AFTER-LIFE

THE after-life is a notion received from religious teaching ; there is no way of establishing its truth save by way of religious dogma and acceptance of the prophets' reports as true ; these refer to what will befall the body at the resurrection, and those corporeal delights or torments which are too well known to require restating here. The true religion brought into this world by our Prophet Muhammad has described in detail the state of happiness or misery awaiting us hereafter so far as the body is concerned. Some further support for the idea of a hereafter is attainable through reason and logical demonstration—and this is confirmed by prophetic teaching—namely, that happiness or misery posited by spiritual appraisement ; though it is true that our conjecture falls short of realizing a full picture of them now, for reasons which we shall explain. Metaphysicians have a greater desire to achieve this spiritual happiness than the happiness which is purely physical ; indeed they scarcely heed the latter, and were they granted it would not consider it of great moment in comparison with the former kind, which is proximity to the First Truth, in a manner to be described presently. Let us therefore consider this state of happiness, and of contrasting misery : the physical sort is fully dealt with in the teachings of religion.

Every faculty of the soul has its own particular pleasure and good, its own especial pain and evil. For example, pleasure and good as appertaining to the appetite consists in the realization of a congenial sensual state through the senses ; pleasure in relation to choler is the achievement of mastery ; pleasure in terms of the imagination is the sensation of hope ; the pleasure of memory is the reminiscence of agreeable circumstances that happened in the past. Pain in each case is the opposite of the corresponding pleasure. All of these have one feature in common, that consciousness of agreeable and congenial circumstances which constitutes the good and pleasure of each. What is essentially and really agreeable to each is the realization of a sense of fulfilment which is relatively speaking the achievement in actuality of its potential perfection.

While the various faculties have these features in common, in reality they differ among themselves in degree : one kind of perfection is completer and more excellent, another is quantitively greater, another is more enduring, another is more readily attainable. The sort which is in actuality more perfect and excellent, and is in itself more intense in realization, of course involves a more exquisite and satisfying pleasure.

Moreover it may happen in the actualization of some sorts of perfection that the perfection is known to exist and to be pleasurable, but that its state cannot be pictured in the mind, nor the pleasure connected with it sensed until the state itself is realized ; and that which cannot be sensed consciously is not desired or yearned after. Thus, while an impotent man may be quite convinced that intercourse is pleasurable, yet he does not desire and long for it in the manner peculiar to that sensation but with quite another appetite—like that of a man who is experimenting to discover how a certain sensation may be achieved, even if it be in fact painful : in short, he cannot imagine it at all. Similar is the state of the blind man in relation to beautiful forms, or of the deaf in regard to melodious tunes.

Hence it behoves not the intelligent man to suppose that every pleasure is connected with the belly and the sexual instinct, as is the case with asses ; that the First Principles, which dwell in close proximity to the Lord of All, are wholly without pleasure and exultation ; or that Almighty God in His Sublime Splendour and Infinite Power does not enjoy a State of Noble Pre-eminence and Well-being which we reverently refrain from calling pleasure. Asses and wild beasts have it is true their own sort of well-being and pleasure ; but what relation is there between these mean delights, and the sensation enjoyed by the Lofty Principles ? Their beatitude we may only imagine and contemplate : we cannot know it in our conscient minds, but solely by analogy ; our state being that of the deaf man who never in all his life heard or could imagine the joy of music, yet he was sure that it was truly excellent.

It can further happen that perfection and absolute congeniality may be within the reach of the apprehending faculty, but there is some impediment or preoccupation in the soul which causes it to hate that perfection and to prefer its opposite. Thus, a sick man will sometimes hate wholesome food and desire only the unwholesome, which is essentially detestable ; or one may not actually hate a certain perfection, but merely lack all sense of pleasure in it ; as when a man much afraid secures a triumph or a pleasure of some sort but is not aware of the fact, and feels no pleasure in it.

Again, the apprehending faculty may be atrophied by that which is the opposite of its perfection and so not sense or recoil from its state until, when the obstacle is removed, it is pained by the realization of its situation and so reverts to its normal condition. A bilious person may not be aware of the acidity in him until his temperament is restored and his members healed ; only then will he recoil from the condition which has befallen him. Similarly an animal may have no appetite for food at all and may positively dislike it, though it is the most suitable thing it can have, and continue so for a long time ; but when the obstacle is removed it will return to its natural course of feeling violently hungry, and have so great an appetite for food that it cannot endure to be without it, and will perish if it cannot find any. One can be exposed to conditions causing great pain, such as burning or freezing, yet because the senses are impaired the body may not feel any discomfort until the injury is repaired ; then it will feel the severe pain.

Having established the foregoing principles, we may now return to our immediate object.

Now the peculiar perfection towards which the rational soul strives is that it should become as it were an intellectual micro-cosm, impressed with the form of the All, the order intelligible in the All, and the good pervading the All : first the Principle of the All, then proceeding to the Noble Substances and Absolute Spirituality, then Spirituality connected in some fashion with corporeal things, then the Celestial Bodies with their various dispositions and powers, and so continuing until it realizes com-pletely within itself the shape of all Being, and thus converts itself into an intelligible cosmos of its own in correspondence with the whole existing Cosmos, contemplating perfect Come-liness, absolute Good and true Beauty, and united therewith. So it will have become graven after its idea and pattern, and strung upon its thread as a pearl is strung upon a necklace, being refashioned into the self-same substance thereof.

When this state is compared with those other perfections so ardently beloved of the other faculties, it will be found to be of an order so exalted as to make it seem monstrous to describe it as more complete or more excellent than they ; indeed, there is no relation between it and them whatsoever, whether it be of excellence, completeness, abundance, or any other of the respects wherein delight in sensual attainment is consummated. For if it be a question of durability, how shall eternal continuance be compared with changefulness and corruptibility ? Or if it be a matter of the degree of accomplishment, how can the accomplishment of surface contact be measured against that of penetrating into the very substance of the recipient, so that it is as if the twain are one without any division whatsoever ? For intelligence, intelligible and intelligent are one thing, or nearly so. That the object so apprehended is more perfect in itself is manifest at once ; that the realization too is more intense is likewise immediately obvious, if the foregoing argument is kept at all in mind.

The rational soul has far more numerous objects to apprehend, and is far more strenuous in seeking out its object and isolating it from those accretions which affect not its real meaning save accidentally : it is able to penetrate the object of its apprehension both internally and externally. How indeed can the two sorts of apprehension be at all compared, or this spiritual pleasure be measured against the other sensual, bestial, choleric pleasure ? But we within our world and body, plunged as we are into all kinds of abomination, do not sense that other pleasure even when any of the means of attaining it are within our power ; so we have already indicated above. Consequently we do not seek or yearn after that at all, save indeed if we have torn from our necks the yoke of appetite, anger and their sister passions, and so catch a glimpse of that higher pleasure. Even so, the image we perceive is but faint and feeble, and then only at a time when all our entanglements are loosened and our eyes are strained towards the precious objects of our quest. Our delight before and after may then be thought to stand in the same relation to each other as the sensual delight in inhaling the odours of delicious foods compared with the delight of tasting them ; indeed, the contrast is infinitely greater.

You yourself know how, when you are meditating some abstruse matter that engages you, and then some sensual appetite supervenes, and you are constrained to choose between the two competing interests, you pay no heed to that appetite, if you be a man of noble spirit. Even common spirits too will deny chance lusts and prefer terrible pains and frightful sufferings, because they are ashamed of being exposed to disgrace or opprobrium, or because they are eager for some signal triumph. All these are intellectual states ; some of them are preferred above natural influences, and for their sake natural discomforts will be endured. From this it is realized that intellectual ends are more ennobling to the soul than other worthless things ; how far exceeding then those pure and lofty objects of the spirit ! But mean souls sense only the good and evil that are attached to worthless things, and perceive not the circumstances attending noble objects, because of the impediments already stated.

When the time comes for us to be separated from the body, and our soul has become aware while still in the body of that perfection which is the object of its love, yet has not attained it, though naturally still yearning after it, for it has in fact realized that it exists though its preoccupation with the body has caused it to forget its own essence and its true beloved (and so sickness will cause us to forget the need of replacing the parts that are dissolved within us, or even the pleasure of sweet things and the appetite for them ; and unnatural desire will make a sick man incline after revolting things)—then at that time our soul is truly affected by pain at the loss of our cherished object, equal to the supervening pleasure whose existence we have proved and whose lofty rank we have indicated. This then is a misery and a torment far exceeding the bodily pain and physical anguish of burning and freezing. At that moment we are like to a man who has been drugged, or so affected by fire or cold that the material clothing his senses prevents him from feeling anything, so that he senses no discomfort for the while ; but then the intervening obstacle is removed, and he is conscious of great suffering. If, however, the intellectual faculty has achieved such a degree of perfection within the soul that the latter is able, on leaving the body, to realize that full perfection which lies within its power to attain, the soul will then resemble a man drugged who is given to taste some most delicious food, or confronting him a most ravishing situation, without his being conscious of the fact ; when the drug passes off, he discovers great pleasure all at once. But the pleasure enjoyed by the soul at that moment is not at all of the order of sensual or animal delight ; rather does it resemble that delectable state which belongs to pure vital substances, mightier and nobler than all other pleasure. This then is the happiness, and that the misery which await every soul at death.

Now this misery does not come upon every man who is any way wanting ; rather is it the portion of those who have invested their intellectual faculty with the yearning to achieve perfection. This happens when it has become conclusive to them that it is the business of the soul to apprehend the very essence of perfection, by attaining through knowledge the unknown and striving to actualize its potential perfection. This is no natural and inborn property of the soul, nor indeed of any of the faculties ; on the contrary, most of the faculties become conscious of their respective perfections only as a result of certain causes.

Simple, unsophisticated souls and faculties are as it were mere objectified matter, and never acquire this yearning ; for this yearning only occurs, and is graven upon the substance of the soul, when it is conclusively proved to the spiritual faculties that there are certain matters, the knowledge of which they can acquire in the processes of logic. Otherwise there is no yearning in the soul for these far heights ; yearning follows upon opinion, and opinion such as this belongs not *a priori* to the soul but is acquired. So when these men acquire this opinion, this yearning necessarily attaches to their souls ; if their souls depart out of the body not having as yet acquired that state which will bring them after separation from the flesh to completion, they fall into this sort of everlasting wretchedness ; for the elements of the faculty of knowledge were only to be acquired through the body, and now the body has passed away. Such men are either incapable of the effort required to achieve human perfection, or else they are obstinate, unbelieving, fanatically attached to wrong opinions contrary to the true ; and the unbelieving are in the worst case of all, having acquired dispositions diametrically opposed to perfection.

As for the question how far the human soul needs to be capable of conceiving intelligible abstractions, so that it may pass beyond the point where this misery is bound to befall, and in transgressing which that happiness may be justly hoped for : this is a matter upon which I can only pronounce approximately. I suppose this position is reached when a man achieves a true mental picture of the incorporeal principles, and believes in them implicitly because he is aware of their existence through logical demonstration. He is acquainted with the final causes of events happening in universal (not partial), infinite movements ; he has a firm grasp of the disposition of the All, the mutual proportions of its parts, and the order pervading the Cosmos from the First Principle down to the remotest beings, all duly arranged. He can apprehend Providence in action, and realizes what kind of being belongs exclusively to the Essence Preceding All, what sort of Unity that Essence possesses, how that Essence achieves cognition without any consequent multiplicity or change of any kind, in what manner other beings are related in due order to that Essence.   The clearer the inward vision of the speculative becomes, the more fully qualified he is to attain supreme happiness.

A man will hardly free himself from this world and its entanglements, except he be more firmly attached to the other world, so that his yearning to be gone thither and his love for what awaits him there block him from turning back to gaze at what lies behind him.

I would add, that this true happiness cannot be consummated save by amending the practical part of the soul.   Character, as I have remarked elsewhere, is a " habit " whereby certain actions issue out of the soul easily and without prior deliberation. Aristotle in his books of ethics lays it down that we should observe the Mean between two opposing characteristics, and not that we should strive to make our individual actions conform to the Mean : we must acquire the habit of the Mean.   Now this habit of the Mean appears to belong to both the rational and the animal faculties : to the latter, through acquiring the disposition to submit and be passive, and to the former, through acquiring the disposition to dominate.   Similarly the habits of excess and shortcoming belong equally to the rational and the animal faculties, but in an inverse relationship.   It is well known that excess and shortcoming are necessary features of the animal faculties ; when the animal faculty is strong, and it acquires the habit of domination, the rational soul finds itself disposed to submit ; once passivity becomes ingrained in the rational soul, it strengthens its attachment and confirms its subservience to the body.   The habit of the Mean aims to liberate the rational soul from all disposition to yield, to maintain it in its natural state, and to endow it moreover with the disposition to dominate and to defy—an attitude which is by no means contrary to its true substance, or apt to incline it towards the body, but rather away from it : always the Mean plucks the rational soul from the two extremes.

As for the true substance of the soul, it is the body which overwhelms it and diverts it, causing it to forget its proper yearning and its quest for perfection ; it kills within it all sense of pleasure in that perfection should it ever achieve it, or of the pain of imperfection when falling short of its goal. It is not the case that the soul is as it were ingrained and submerged in the body : the bond which unites body and soul—that natural yearning of the soul to control the body and its preoccupation with the body's exploits, the crises that it brings upon itself, and the habits which become fixed in it—this bond has its origin in the body.

When a man departs this life having within him the habits resulting from his union with the body, he is in a state closely similar to that which was his while still in the body. As that state diminishes, he becomes correspondingly less heedless of the motion of yearning after perfection ; to the degree that it remains with him, he continues veiled from absolute union with the place wherein his happiness resides, so that he is affected by confused motions which prove exceedingly painful.

Such a bodily disposition is contrary to the very substance of the soul, and is injurious to its substance ; the body, and the soul's complete immersion therein, diverts the soul from all consciousness of itself. When the soul leaves the body it senses that mighty opposition and is greatly pained by it ; yet that pain, that anguish is not due to any necessary circumstance but is the result of an accidental contingency, and as such is not permanent and everlasting. It passes away and is nullified with the abandonment of those actions whose repetition strengthened that disposition ; so that it follows that the torment resulting from this circumstance is not eternal, but passes away and is obliterated little by little until the soul is purified and attains its proper happiness.

As for those foolish souls which have never acquired the yearning for perfection, yet leave the body without having acquired any vicious bodily disposition, these pass to the wide Mercy of God and attain a kind of ease. If, however, they have acquired some vicious bodily disposition and have no other condition but that, nothing within them to oppose or strive with it, then they continue inevitably to be bemused by their yearning after what is for them an absolute necessity, and are exquisitely tortured by the loss of the body and all the body's requirements without being able to attain the object of their desire. For the instrument of their desire has been destroyed, while the habit of attachment to the body still survives.

It may also be true, as some theologians state, that when souls, supposing they are pure, leave the body, having firmly fixed within them some such beliefs regarding the future life as are appropriate to them, being the sort of picture which can properly be presented to the ordinary man—when such men as these leave the body, lacking both the force to draw them upwards to complete perfection (so that they achieve that supreme happiness) and likewise the yearning after such perfection (so that they experience that supreme misery), but all their spiritual dispositions are turned towards the lower world and drawn to the corporeal ; since there is nothing to prevent celestial matter from being operable to the action of any soul upon it, these souls may well imagine all those after-life circumstances in which they believed as actually taking place before them, the instrument reinforcing their imagination being some kind of celestial body.

In this way these pure souls will really be spectators of the events of the grave and the resurrection about which they were told in this world, and all the good things of the after-life ; while the wicked souls will similarly behold, and suffer, the punishment which was portrayed to them here below. Certainly the imaginative picture is no weaker than the sensual image ; rather is it the stronger and clearer of the two. This may be observed in dreams : the vision seen in sleep is often of greater moment in its kind than the impression of the senses. The image contemplated in the after-life is however more stable than that seen in dreams, because there are fewer obstacles in the way of its realization ; the soul being isolated from the body, the receiving instrument is therefore absolutely clear. As you know, the image seen in dreams and that sensed in waking are alike simply impressed upon the soul ; they differ only in this, that the former kind originates from within and descends into the soul, while the latter sort originates from without and mounts up into the soul. It is when the image has already been impressed upon the soul that the act of contemplation is consummated. It is this impression, then, that in reality pleases or pains the soul, not any external object ; whatever is impressed upon the soul does its work, even if there be no external cause. The essential cause is the impression itself ; the external object is the accidental cause, or the cause of the cause.

These then are the baser sorts of celestial happiness and misery, which are apposite to base souls. As for the souls of the blessed, they are far removed from such circumstances ; being perfect, they are united to the Essence, and are wholly plunged in true pleasure ; they are forever free of gazing after what lies behind them, and the kingdom that once was theirs. If there had remained within them any trace of those things, whether by reason of dogmatic belief or through acceptance of a physical

F

theory, they would be so injured thereby as to fall short of scaling the topmost peak of heaven, until that thing be finally obliterated from their souls.

(From the *Kitāb al-Najāt*.)

POEM OF THE SOUL

Out of her lofty home she hath come down
Upon thee, this white dove in all the pride
Of her reluctant beauty ; veiled is she
From every eye eager to know her, though
In loveliness unshrouded radiant.
Unwillingly she came, and yet perchance
Still more unwilling to be gone from thee ;
So she is torn by griefs. First she refrained,
Being all unaccustomed ; but at last,
When she was firmly knit, she loved the use
Of being neighbour to this arid waste.
And now methinks she hath forgotten quite
The tents where once she dwelt, the far abodes
She was so little satisfied to leave.
So, being now united with these depths
And parted from her sandy hills of yore,
Her wings are heavy upon her, and she rests
Dejected mid these waymarks and mean mounds
Weeping (yet she remembereth not her home
Of yore), until her tears abundant flow,
And she not yet set forth. But when the time
Is nigh for her departing to that place
And near the hour to be upon her way
Unto the broader plain, then perching high
Upon the topmost steep, she carolleth—
For knowledge doth uplift the lowliest heart—
With ken of every hidden mystery

In all the world returning, still unstopped
The orifice of heeding ; and it proves
Her coming down was necessary woe
That she might list to truth else all unheard.
Why then was she cast down from her high peak
To this degrading depth ? God brought her low,
But for a purpose wise, that is concealed
E'en from the keenest mind and liveliest wit.
And if the tangled mesh impeded her,
The narrow cage denied her wings to soar
Freely in heaven's high ranges, after all
She was a lightning-flash that brightly glowed
Momently o'er the tents, and then was hid
As though its gleam was never glimpsed below.

INDEX

INDEX